D0439731

I, Carmelita Tropicana

I, Carmelita Tropicana

Performing Between Cultures

Alina Troyano

with Ela Troyano and Uzi Parnes

edited by Chon A. Noriega

Beacon Press Boston

Beacon Press
25 Beacon Street
Boston, Massachusetts 02108-2892
www.beacon.org

Beacon Press books
are published under the auspices of
the Unitarian Universalist Association of Congregations.

Printed in the United States of America
05 04 03 02 01 00 8 7 6 5 4 3 2 1
This book is printed on
recycled acid-free paper that contains
at least 20 percent postconsumer waste and meets
the uncoated paper ANSI/NISO specifications for
permanence as revised in 1992.
Text design by Julia Sedykh Design
Composition by Wilsted & Taylor Publishing Services

Copyright acknowledgments appear on page 196.

Library of Congress Cataloging-in-Publication Data
Troyano, Alina.
I, Carmelita Tropicana : performing between cultures / Alina
Troyano with Ela Troyano and Uzi Parnes ; edited by Chon A. Noriega.
p. cm.
ISBN 0-8070-6603-6 (pbk.)
1. Cuban American women Drama. 2. Lesbians—United States Drama.
I. Troyano, Ela. II. Parnes, Uzi. III. Noriega, Chon A., 1961– IV. Title.
PS3570.R698 I23 2000
812′.54—dc21
99-35624

For all my families

especially my sister Ela who made this book possible

Contents

Editor's Introduction: Very Good with the Tongue

"Hello people, you know me, I know you. I am Carmelita Tropicana. I say Loisaida is the place to be. It is multicultural, multinational, multigenerational, mucho multi. And like myself, you've got to be multilingual. I am very good with the tongue."

Very good, indeed. These lines from the screenplay *Carmelita Tropicana: Your Kunst Is Your Waffen* reveal the method behind the apparent madness of Alina Troyano's performance alter ego, Carmelita Tropicana. That method: When two or more cultural systems come into contact—and when don't they?—the best survival strategy consists of finding the "multi" that holds them together in communication. For Troyano, that "multi" is language itself, but it is a language that is always imprecise, especially when working between national cultures, political frameworks, or sexual orientations. Multi, multi, multi.

One necessarily comes to know both Alina Troyano and Carmelita Tropicana through innuendo, bilingual puns, double entendre, burlesque parody, political farce, biographical revisionism, and an irreverent appropriation and collaging of popular culture. Chicken sushi, anyone? How about a German-Spanish-English medley? But consider the title of this book, too. It declares "I, Carmelita Tropicana" with an almost Cartesian certitude. But its two homonyms point in another direction, revealing the reaction of others to the self-proclaimed identity. The first homonym registers shock, exasperation, or sexual pleasure as an interpersonal expression ("Aiiiiy, Carmelita Tropicana"); the second conjures up the flip side of identity, the act of being seen and identified, the surveillance imperative that emerges alongside the liberal notion of identity in the modern era ("Eye Carmelita Tropicana"). Identity is no simple matter here: what the self proclaims, another both authenticates and challenges by the very fact of a response, while the state and marketplace "eye" this interaction for their own purposes. There is not one Carmelita Tropicana, but three! Which raises a question about the author. . . .

Alina Troyano was born in Cuba before the revolution and came to the United States as a child in the early 1960s. In short, she is a member of what Gustavo Pérez Firmat calls the "1.5 generation," born on the island but raised in the United States. It is a generation whose "exile" is lived through their parents' memories and modified by American mass culture.[1] We next hear about Troyano in 1982, when she stepped into the East Village performance scene, along with Holly Hughes, and both women quickly became regulars.[2] Within the first year, Hughes organized Troyano's first performance, a fashion show, and cast her in Hughes's own *The Well of Horniness*.

Yet Troyano found it difficult to be on stage as herself, as Alina, and soon developed Carmelita Tropicana, a bold synthesis of cubanidad (Cuban-ness), lesbian sexuality, and female spectacle. But not without collaborators: Uzi Parnes and her sister Ela Troyano. Together all three developed the Tropicana character and performances. Ela Troyano, a protégé of Jack Smith, was also actively involved in the multimedia and experimental film scene; she and Parnes also ran Club Chandalier, which provided the venue for Alina's popular talk show, *Cheet Chat with Carmelita*. Through the figure of Carmelita Tropicana, Alina Troyano brought together the seemingly incompatible parts of her life: the "1.5 generation" and the "queer frontier."[3] Performance became the arena within which Latino culture and lesbian identity could speak to each other in ways that challenged each's underlying myth. As José Esteban Muñoz argues, her work combines two male-dominated linguistic tropes: gay camp and Cuban choteo (mockery). "No one is let off the hook: the ironic and sharp attacks on Cuban and Cuban American racism, sexism, and general hypocrisy are not retracted."[4] But what makes Troyano's work unique is that its political sensibility both critiques and embraces. Multi, multi, multi. In the process, lesbian identity becomes the center of Cuban nationalism, even as it also struggles against the authoritarian state, cubanidad, and the U.S. blockade of Cuba!

In *Memories of the Revolution,* Troyano reworks two Cuban nationalist allegories in order to situate Carmelita Tropicana at their center. Act II offers a re-enactment of la Virgen del Cobre's appearance before three adrift Cuban sailors (black, white, and mulatto), an act that offered a symbolic resolution to the racial divisions that marked the nation. Here, however, the three sailors are two Cuban lesbians and a German female spy, and the time period is adjusted to correlate the Cuban Revolution and the emergence of U.S. performance art in the happenings. When la Virgen appears, she informs Carmelita that she must give up the Cuban Revolution for an international one aimed at women, telling her in a mixture of English and German, "Your kunst is your waffen." The phrase carries vague sexual overtones, but translates as "Your art is your weapon." La Virgen further informs Carmelita that she will be granted eternal youth provided she never lets a man touch her, to which Carmelita replies, ". . . that is never to be a problem."

The second nationalist allegory is referenced in the title itself, which suggests Tomás Gutiérrez Alea's *Memories of Underdevelopment* (1968), the first major feature film produced in postrevolutionary Cuba. The film concerns itself with the role of the nonrevolutionary, postbourgeoise artist amid the Cuban missile crisis—and it does so by juxtaposing the main character's sex life and psychological observations with an apocalyptic moment as the new state found itself at the center of the cold war.

It is within these two allegories that Troyano replaces the earnest males of the originals and inserts none other than Carmelita Tropicana: self-proclaimed "songbird of Cuba," revolutionary, beauty queen, intellectual, superintendent, and performance artiste. But what secures this displacement is another figure in Troyano's repertoire: Pingalito Betancourt, conductor of the M15 bus and something of a street philosopher on all things Cuban. Pingalito, slang for Little Penis, delivers a choteo on Cuban nationalism, but he also recites the more celebratory "Ode to the Cuban Man" and waxes poetic over Tongolele's behind. In these respects, he is not that different from the main character in Gutiérrez Alea's film. Both provide lectures, criticism, and lyricism in equal measure; and in both the imbrication of sexual and political discourses complicate the parody. But if Pingalito—performed by Troyano in drag—is a Latino macho par excellence, he also adores Carmelita Tropicana. It is he who identifies a lesbian chanteuse as the "symbol of Cuban womanhood." This archetypal macho stands witness to a past and memory that he never had—the lo que tenía (what I used to have [before the revolution]) of exilic memory—but that he reveres nonetheless. This dynamic produces a performance that interrelates nationality, gender, and sexuality without reducing them to a single point of identification, "Cuban lesbian artist." Instead, Troyano stresses the "multi, multi, multi" that brings together Latino, queer, and arts audiences (not to mention the inevitable admixtures) in a way that remains unpredictable and multivalent. For her, "all these shifts of identity depend upon who is doing the seeing."[5] Not everyone is the same. More recently, with *Milk of Amnesia,* Troyano has added her own autobiographical voice to her performance. Even so, she turns from the personal to the political—in large part by subtly merging Carmelita and Alina in the closing lines in order to call for an end to the blockade. More to the point, however, Troyano makes her appeal on the basis of a unity rooted in colonialism—which is to say, othering—rather than humanism.

Troyano's work compares with that of other well-known performance artists who use identity as a way to foreground and examine cultural difference (Guillermo Gómez-Peña, Coco Fusco, James Luna), sexuality (Luís Alfaro, Karen Finley, Tim Miller, Annie Sprinkle, Holly Hughes), and postmodernity (Laurie Anderson, Harry Gamboa, Jr.). What makes Troyano unique is that she works in all three registers with a linguistic playfulness that is as irreverent as it is insightful. In her most recent performance, *Chicas 2000,* Troyano offers a futurist fantasy about identity and commodification, depicting the havoc caused by unauthorized cloning from Carmelita Tropicana's buttocks! This collection brings together Troyano's major performance scripts, a screenplay (co-authored and directed by her sister Ela Troyano), and several shorter performances and essays. These works place race and ethnicity into play with gender and sexuality. But rather than define a uniquely composite identity (that is, base her authority on being a Cuban lesbian artist), Troyano prefers to be "very good with the tongue," using language to conjure up the multiple characters and social relations that define America at the end of the millennium.

1. See José Esteban Muñoz, "No es fácil: Notes on the Negotiation of Cubanidad and Exilic Memory in Carmelita Tropicana's *Milk of Amnesia,*" *The Drama Review* 39, no. 3 (1995): 76–82.
2. "Carmelita Tropicana Unplugged," interview by David Román, *ibid.,* 84.
3. C. Carr, "The Queer Frontier," in C. Carr, *On Edge: Performance at the End of the Twentieth Century* (Middletown, CT: Wesleyan University Press, 1993), 84–87.
4. José Esteban Muñoz, "Choteo/Camp Style Politics: Carmelita Tropicana's Performance of Self-Enactment," *Women and Performance: A Journal of Feminist Theory* 7, no. 2–8, no. 1 (1995): 38–51, see 44.
5. "Carmelita Tropicana Unplugged," 90.

Author's Introduction

The pen is the tongue of the mind. Did I say that? No, it was that other linguist Miguel de Cervantes. I, Carmelita, say:

Hello people you know me I know you
I don't need no American Express card
Ich bin schoenheitzkonigin
Reina de belleza de Loisaida
Carmelita Tropicana
Ms. Lower East Side Beauty Queen
Famous nightclub entertainer
Superintendent and performance artiste

I love to be a performance artist because you get to travel a lot. And I have a talent that is very good for traveling. I pick languages up pretty fast. First there was Spanish in Cuba where I was born and then English in America where I got reared. And of course on my first international tour of Germany I pick up the language the Deutsche and a lot more—I pick up Kunst, Art.

IN SEARCH OF KUNST

NYC, downtown, the eighties. That is when I first began my search for Kunst.

A happy fun time for artists, playful, innocent; there was enough money for an artist to make art, survive, hang out. Clubs and art galleries flourished. It was the best of times: Art was more about process than product, more about esthetic edification than career, more about transgression than mainstream assimilation. It was the worst of times:

AIDS hit, clubs and galleries closed, the NEA started defunding, the culture wars began.

But to go back to the happy times when my life changed. It happened one night at the Women's One World (WOW) International Festival, held in multiple venues on the Lower East Side. My eyes were ablaze at the spectacle of so many women in all colors, sizes, shapes doing every art imaginable—music, poetry, theatre, cooking. I thought I'd found paradise. I was especially moved by the play *Split Britches*, performed by a theatre troupe with the same name, made up of Deb Margolin, Peggy Shaw, and Lois Weaver. As the future Carmelita would exclaim: It made me cry in one eye and laugh in the other. At last, feministas with a sense of humor! I was hooked. So when the girls that put the Festival together opened up the WOW cafe, I followed.

THERE'S A PLACE FOR US

I became a member of WOW, a loose collective of wayward girls, mostly lesbians, a place that offered an artistic salon on East 11th Street. There were art exhibits, poetry readings, variety nights, thematic parties like the Military Drag Ball and the XXX-Rated Xmas, workshops in butch, femme, and stand-up comedy. All accompanied by melted brie sandwiches. A place where the credo for everywoman was "Express yourself." A place that said if existing theatre does not represent women like us, let us create that theatre. A place seething with untapped talent.

One such talented member was Holly Hughes, who had written *The Well of Horniness* and cast me as Al Dente, Chief of Police, and Georgette, a butch girl. The role of Al Dente became easier to tackle once Jack Smith, infamous filmmaker and performance artist (who I met through Ela Troyano and Uzi Parnes) admired by many, from Federico Fellini to Nan Goldin, watched the rehearsal and gave me three magic words: Bark the part. Bark the part, of course. I had imagined Al Dente as a cross between Marlon Brando's Godfather and a bulldog. Georgette was harder. Playing butch hit closer to home. All those voices from my adolescence came back to haunt me: "Don't laugh that loud." "Don't walk that way, pareces una carretonera." "You look like a truck driver." I had been sent to charm and etiquette school to cure my gruff demeanor. Now I was being asked to play a butch girl and revel in it. When I stepped on stage, took off my shirt exposing bare arms in a tank T-shirt, and flexed my muscles, the girls went "Oooh." I had a revelation: This wasn't so bad.

It was at the WBAI radio station in the studio, waiting to perform *The Well of Horniness*, that I came up with the name of my alter ego. As the clock showed two minutes before the on-the-air sign was about to go on, my pulse raced and with a rush more euphoric than that from cocaine, I came up with my new name Carmelita and last name Tro—Tropicana. I hit the jackpot.

Now I had a name and the name was especially helpful for the comedy class I was taking at WOW. I had felt too naked and self-conscious to do stand-up; with the name came a character, and the character had red lipstick, a beauty mole, an accent. But what to wear? That was solved when my future collaborators Ela Troyano and Uzi Parnes presented me with their Christmas gift. I opened the box and touched the thick, rich, red velvet cloth with big purple and pink roses, I thought for upholstering my couch, but as I took it out of the box I saw it wasn't for my couch, it was an evening gown. Now I was ready. The moment to strut my stand-up stuff had come. I waited backstage. My teacher signaled me to go on and Carmelita opened her mouth: Hello people.

ETIQUETTE AND ESTHETICS

If WOW had an esthetics it was that of the Ridiculous Theatre and Split Britches. It was camp. It was queer. It was comedy. In fact it was at WOW that I got to see live stand-up for the first time. It was a double bill of Marga Gómez and Reno. So it made sense then for WOW to offer a workshop in stand-up comedy.

The teacher giving the stand-up workshop, although she had a wry sense of humor, was not a counter-culture, downtown type and did not share this sensibility. She was a professional who had been playing comedy clubs and was hardened by the experience of hearing nightly routines full of dumb dick jokes. She thought WOW was too soft a spot, it was not the real world. Her advice focused on how to make it to mainstream and get on *Letterman*. She warned me about using foreign words and expressions that middle America, the target audience, was not familiar with. Chutzpah and oy vey had to go. But the sensuous pleasure I got from rolling meshuggener around my lips and tongue I couldn't give up, or the idea of teaching a vocabulary word, or playing in the backyard of a different culture. My political resistance came in the way of a Jewish poem titled "Oy Vey Number 1."

The teacher was right—WOW was a soft spot embracing gender discourse and that was not the rest of the world. I found that out when I got a gig at the Limelight for a modeling show. They wanted all kinds of street people. I thought I'd go butch. I wore a man's suit, men's shoes, hair slicked back, hung a big gold medallion from my neck and did not wear any lipstick. I looked like a heavy hitter butch Latina who would have been at home at the old La Escuelita on 9th Avenue, full of queens and working-class folks. The reaction I got from the other models in the show was icy. They avoided looking at me. The photographer posed everyone for a group picture and left me out. These people had no etiquette. My teacher was right. She didn't promise me a butch garden. This was the real world.

THERE'S A PLACE FOR US—THE OTHER—AND IT'S UPTOWN

If WOW was a theatre space grounded in gender and sexual politics, Intar was the Latin hood where we could check out our roots. Intar, an arts complex with two spaces—one on 42nd Street and the other on 53rd Street—nurtured Latino talent through its theatre, art gallery, and two significant workshops, the playwriting workshop led by María Irene Fornes and the musical theatre workshop led by George Ferencz and Graciela Daniele. I was chosen to join the musical theatre workshop with a stipend attached. Money for art, that was a novel concept for me. How lucky can a girl get? All I had to do was write the book for a musical. So I agreed and went to ask Lois Weaver of Split Britches what that meant.

It was not easy. I had never written more than a few monologues in the voice of Carmelita. A play seemed a Herculean task. (Xena had not yet arrived). And a musical to boot. I'd only seen one live musical, *Fiddler on the Roof.* I couldn't do it. I tried summoning Chekhov but he would not come. Desperate, I begged María Irene to let me audit a few classes at her lab.

Irene is a formidable teacher as well as La Grande Dame del Teatro. Any Latino writing today has been through Irene and Irene has been through them. The lab began with yoga. After yoga you would get coffee and sit at desks perfectly laid out in a circular shape making sure all desk corners touched. This was very important. She would begin the writing exercises "Close your eyes and . . ." I squinted and saw some people with heads raised like the blind trying to see; others had contorted bodies, but all were concentrating. What I wrote was self-conscious and did not ring true. She advised me that writing was quiet observation. If I imagined that outside it was snowing and there was a man with a snow shovel, the man could be shoveling or not. I had to observe. The man could speak or not. I should not put words into people's mouths but let them speak for themselves. This seemed the opposite of the active comedy writing I was doing. One day I wrote in that quiet way, observing, and reached that deep state of concentration where your surroundings disappear and you go into your writing. After that class in that dreamlike state, outside on the street, a car honk stopped me from getting run over. This was dangerous writing and the kind that would come in handy at a later date; for now I felt inspired.

I went back to the musical theatre workshop and my lab director told me to forget Chekhov and write for Carmelita. So I did and gushed at the thrill of hearing my lyrics set to the ingenious melodies of composer Fernando Rivas.

Like WOW, Intar was significant for the network it provided. It was there I met María Irene, Graciela Daniele, and Max Ferra, as well as other writers and musicians that were starting out, like Manuel Pereiras, Ana María Simo, Lorraine Llamas, Alfredo Bejar, Micky Cruz, Bobby Sanabria, Luis Santeiro. It was here that I was paired up with Fernando Rivas and our styles meshed so well that we became collaborators in and out of Intar. But he was not my first collaborator.

REFLECTIONS THROUGH A CUBAN EYE

My first collaborators were Uzi Parnes and my biological sister Ela Troyano, who are both filmmakers, directors, and writers. To this day I collaborate with each one in some capacity, whether as director, dramaturg, or cowriter. Their artistic generosity allows me to adapt work we have created together and present it as recycled solo performance. They are still the two people I trust most for feedback.

As a triumvirate of two cubists and one Jewish (an Uzi-ism), we created work that made Carmelita the protagonist, a super Latina heroine who, when pitted against evil forces, always triumphed in the end.

Ela and Uzi added a flamboyancy to Carmelita—Uzi by creating fruited boas and hat chandeliers that light up my life and the stage, Ela by saving a charred sequined bustier from a fire I had in my apartment, adding glittered fruit to the burnt left breast so I could appear at a TV interview looking intact with just a hint of smoke. Together they created exquisite visuals in multimedia that made spectacles of our pieces and helped shape the work by providing plot development and narrative structure. As artists both are analytical and versatile enough to mix intellectual semiotics and structural theory with pop culture. But they do have their differences. Uzi is like a painter with a flair for using big extravagant brush strokes; Ela uses finer brush strokes with lots of details. As I see them, Uzi is more attuned to the musical comedy, Ela to the screwball comedy. As directors they begin their approach at opposite ends. They are like belly buttons: Ela is an innie, Uzi an outie. I remember when I asked them to help me with a character I was playing that I felt I had not gotten. Uzi gave me suggestions of physical tasks to do on stage; Ela asked me questions that led me to delve deeper into the character. I found both approaches effective and eventually leading to the same end.

MEMORIES FROM THE CORNERS OF MY MEDULLA OBLONGATA

First times usually occupy a dulce, sweet spot in one's heart. So it is with *Memorias de la Revolución/Memories of the Revolution,* my first play written with Uzi Parnes. *Memorias* was fun to do, was critically well received, and set the tone for my future collaborations with Uzi. As with other works, we took on multiple jobs. Uzi wrote, directed, and designed and I acted, wrote, and helped produce.

We found that an effective shortcut to writing a play was knowing the talent and writing parts for them. At WOW auditions were unthinkable, but there was plenty of talent. We had three of the future Lesbian Brothers: Maureen Angelos, Peggy Healey and Lisa Kron. We knew Peggy and Lisa were not only funny, but could also sing, so we could give them musical numbers. Maureen Angelos was wonderful at male drag and cut a dashing figure that made both straight women and lesbians swoon. She was cast as Carmelita's brother Machito, a recurring character in other plays. Diane Jeep Ries had done a Marlene Dietrich and was good with a German accent; she became our German spy. Holly Hughes and Allison Rooney, fabulous writers and performers, both exuding Americana, played the American tourists. Kate Stafford's performances had a comic edge suited to the Chief of Police, and Quinn added to the cabaret ambience as the cigarette girl and the go-go dancer Dance Machine. Uzi was thrilled at the gender-bending possibilities that an all-female cast, with some playing male roles, would bring.

Besides the obvious reason of the name I had chosen, there were other reasons for setting Act I of *Memorias* at the Tropicana nightclub in Havana 1957. Act III takes place in a replica of the club Tropicana A-Go-Go in New York City in 1967. This suited the narrative as well as eliminated a big set change. For Uzi, who loved musicals, the setting was a chance to stage musical numbers. To create the cabaret environment he set up tables and chairs for the audience. For me the Tropicana conjured up bedtime stories of the greatest nightclub and memories of my relatives, exiles who romantically yearned for a prerevolutionary Cuba.

Like many of the downtown shows of the period, *Memorias* owed much of its color scheme to Material for the Arts, an organization that takes fabric, paints, and all kinds of supplies and furniture from businesses and recycles them for artists. Material for the Arts had bolts of green and orange fabric. Uzi was imaginative with the flaming red-orange lamé and a neon lime-green polyester, using both for the curtains and the costumes. He added a more subdued faux Henri Rousseau as a set backdrop. My stand-up comedy teacher thought it odd and asked why Lisa, who played the chanteuse, was dressed like the curtain. Lisa in turn milked her entrance proudly, pointing to her dress and the curtain.

With *Memorias* we realized the importance of titles and names. *Memorias de la Revolución/Memories of the Revolution* fit symmetrically both English and Spanish. It was grand and ludicrous enough for Carmelita and reminiscent of the great film by Tomás Gutiérrez Alea's *Memorias del Subdesarrollo/Memories of Underdevelopment*. If a title hooked an audience, a name fed the imagination. When I heard the name Pingalito in a conversation, I stole it immediately. Pingalito, little Dick, a typical macho Cubano, sauntered off the page with guayabera and cigar.

Although *Memorias* was a comedy, my favorite moment in the play came from a not-so-funny image I had of someone being tortured to a seductive jazz riff. I told Uzi my image and he turned it into a musical number where Carmelita's protégé and singer Rosita dances with the sadistic Chief of Police, who demands she sing a love song, abusively twisting her arm, pushing her around, and finally dropping her on the floor.

Uzi thought that what *Memorias* was missing was religious iconography. He conceived Act II somewhere near the Bermuda Triangle. Carmelita, who has escaped the revolution, is in a boat with two cohorts, lost at sea. The Virgin could appear to Carmelita, but if she's Jewish and speaks Yiddish, who could we get to play a Yiddish mama? After a storm at sea, Carmelita prays and two little angels open up a triptych in the background, revealing on film the apparition that is Uzi as the Virgin.

COOKING PERFORMANCE ART

I'm like a short-order cook when I make performance art pieces, quickly whipping up a piece for a specific event and audience. When the Dance Critics Association asked me to be on a panel on performance art, I concocted the *Performance Art Manifesto* according to Carmelita. I can then toss the *Manifesto* liberally into other performances, e.g., a performance for the Bad Girls Exhibit at The New Museum of Contemporary Art.

Recipe for Carmelita's Bad Girls Show at The New Museum of Contemporary Art

INGREDIENTS

⅓ Pingalito (Carmelita in male drag) recites
"Ode to the Cuban Man" from Milk of Amnesia
⅓ Carmelita delivers Performance Art Manifesto
⅓ The Art Quiz Show

HOW TO MAKE THE ART QUIZ SHOW

Sprinkle clues for the audience to guess the artwork or artist recreated in live tableaux.
Add a pinch of art commentary to taste and blend with 1 generous dollop of modern dancer Jennifer Monson whisked rapidly for Duchamp's Nude Descending a Staircase.
Set aside.

In a separate pan mix
½ cup of Jennifer as Cupid with piercing arrow and
½ cup of Carmelita moaning, hanging on museum
fire escape
Simmer to Wagner's Tristan und Isolde *and stir*
until both harden into Bernini's sculpture
The Agony of St. Theresa.
Set aside.

In separate bowl create the crème fraîche of one of the
baddest girl artists beaten into soft peaks until stiff but
not dry, a half-and-half bisexual, add to it the fuzzy
peach of one who disdains depilatories and plucking
and lace it with 80 percent proof mezcal, garnish with
sugar skulls and candied flowers for an artist who can
withstand excruciating pain and paint and paint
because art is her life and Kunst is supreme Frida Kahlo.
One hundred percent artist.
Buen Provecho and Bon Appétit

CH CH CH CH CH CHANGES

The gloom of the latter part of the eighties spilled onto the new decade. The effects of the AIDS epidemic were devastating the arts community, the economy took a nose dive, homelessness was on the rise, the culture wars took their toll on artists and arts organizations, and everyone scrambled to survive.

For me the nineties was a period of transition. The Parnes-Troyano-Tropicana trio dissolved and we all produced work independently. I took on more work as an actress and solo artist and, prompted by "The Decade Show," I began experimenting with a different style of writing.

"The Decade Show: Frameworks of Identity in the 1980s," a collaboration of three museums (The New Museum of Contemporary Art, the Museum of Contemporary Hispanic Art, and the Studio Museum of Harlem), brought together curators, artists, and critics to examine representative "nonmainstream or oppositional art" and provide an understanding of the period. As an artist asked to perform, I began to take stock of the work I'd been creating, and this inevitably led to the question, "What's next?"

My performance at "The Decade Show" was a collage of old and new work. I adapted excerpts from *Memorias de la Revolución, The Boiler Time Machine,* and *Candela* and seized the opportunity to write more personal autobiographical monologues. But without the Carmelita fruits I felt naked, which is why I did the monologues in the dark, for after all, as a born and bred ex-Catholic our confessions take place in the dark.

REMEMBER WALKING IN THE SAND?

I once read that the act of remembering is like xerox copying. You remember a memory, and then the next time you remember it's the memory of the memory you are remembering, and after that it's the memory of the memory of the memory, and so on. My trip to Cuba as an adult in 1993 brought back many memories and gave me the topic for my solo *Milk of Amnesia. Milk* was conceived as if inside the brain; when you tapped a certain area, a memory would unfold.

Ela, who acted as director and dramaturg, was invaluable in the creation and development of the piece. She urged me to combine the more personal autobiographical style with the campy satire of earlier work. With Milk my schizophrenia blossomed, and I was able to combine the voice of Carmelita with mine, that of the writer, and sprinkle it with assorted animals whose voices gave us a glimpse of Cuban history.

Unlike earlier, more colorful and flamboyant work, Ela wanted *Milk* to be subdued, intimate, and she suggested we hire Kukuli Velarde, a Peruvian sculptor, to design the show.

One of the most exhilarating times in the collaborative process is when you get together with your collaborators, kicking ideas around, and you watch as these ideas evolve and get incorporated into the show. The images of milk and childhood memories in the text were embodied in the visuals. Kukuli translated milk and amnesia into white; she wanted everything painted white, including the theatre. This had to be scaled down at Performance Space 122, where we premiered the show, to a white cube and white costume. The three of us started to free associate childhood images and came up with balloons. I told them I'd visited a friend in the hospital who had a brain injury and had wires attached to her head resembling a hat. Kukuli created a hat with white balloons which Carmelita wears in the hospital sequence when she is suffering from amnesia. Kukuli and I proposed helium ballons in the hat so it could ascend upwards. Ela pops our balloon and comes up with the next image: piñata. She tells us one of the most memorable performances she has seen was Jack Smith's adaptation of Ibsen's *Ghosts,* where a little stuffed animal went across the stage and spilled glitter from its body. Kukuli sculpts a six-foot papier-mâché pig with the face of one who is about to be slaughtered. Just like the piñata bursts open and candy spills on the ground, so too, our pig had a tampon. When it was pulled, glitter gushed from its neck, forming a puddle of glittered blood on the white linoleum floor. The red glitter blood is a stolen homage to Jack Smith.

Milk is the show I have toured the most, but as with all touring, since presenting organizations vary in terms of space and resources, one must improvise. Alas, the pig, though magnificent at six feet, is too difficult as a traveling companion. In Barcelona the pig substitute was a whole ham serrano, in London it was can of Spam, and in Los Angeles a two-foot-tall Mexican piggy bank.

IN THE YEAR 2017 WILL CHICAS BE ALIVE?

Chicas 2000 had a lot in common with *Memorias.* I had a cast, a director, and a booking, and had to write a press release before there was a play. Ellie Covan of Dixon Place got us commissioning funds from the Joyce Mertz Gilmore Foundation and booked it for June as part of the Toyota Comedy Festival. Since *Chicas* was part of the festival it had to be funny, and since we were in mid-March I had to write pronto.

At the time I wanted to set aside solo work and longed for a bigger show like *Memorias;* I longed to gather live girls on stage with me. It was also around that time that Dolly was cloned and the scientific possibilities gripped me.

My cast was made up of Rebecca Sumner Burgos and Ana Margaret Sánchez, young, tall, voluptuous latinas. I thought, What if Carmelita was cloned and Ana and Rebecca were her clones? That worked for me.

I had to be very fertile with so close a deadline and this is when everything becomes grist for the mill. I heard a greeting on my answering machine: "Oye, chusma." It was the affectionate greeting of José Muñoz, NYU professor of Performance Studies. Chusma. The word is used in Latin America and it means loud, tacky, excessive behavior and tastes associated with "lower classes." The American equivalent of chusma is bottom feeder, white trailer trash, except that this is people-of-color trash. I married cloning to chusma and came up with the premise of the show. Carmelita, who has the chusma gene, a gene deemed harmful to society, is cloned by the stalking wanna-be chusma, Dr. Igor. To cure her disease a futuristic society has created jails known as Behavior Modification Units, where Carmelita and her clones are interned.

I thought meeting informally with the cast would get my creative juices going. I asked them if they had a fantasy of doing something on stage, what would that be. Uzi said he wanted to direct but also wanted to play a small role. Ana Margaret said she wanted to use her body in odd ways, to express herself physically, not necessarily through dance. Rebecca talked about cannibalism, its meaning and necessity, both metaphorically and not, and said she also wanted to sing a song. I tried honoring their wish list. Uzi got to play the mad scientist, Dr. Igor. Ana got to use her legs as the hands of a giant clock opening and closing in a musical number. Rebecca got a monologue about her urges to eat human fingers ("They don't even need hot sauce").

We were very lucky to have Charles Scott Richards as the designer for *Chicas* at both Dixon Place and Performance Space 122.

PERSONA GRATA AND NOT

It is hard to believe, but I've encountered times when Carmelita has been persona non grata. It must have been las frutas, which Enrique Fernández, a critic, referred to as "dangerous fruits." Those dangerous fruits had been my collaborator's signature piece and pièce de résistance.

It was after my performance at "The Decade Show" that my girlfriend of two months, a politically liberal woman, confessed to me that the fruits I wore made her ill. Latina stereotype, she thought. But now she understood and liked what she saw on stage. The same happened to a photographer I met at the taping of the TV show *Cristina* on nightclubs in New York City. Carmelita's topics ranged from real estate on the Lower East Side of New York City to performance art and finally nightclubs, as I recalled the night at a nightclub called MK's where I met Donny the human horse, who wore a saddle and gave me a ride. The photographer said when he saw the fruits he thought I was a crazy stupid woman, but after listening to me talk he liked what I had to say.

And there was that other incident that caused me to ponder how the persona is received. It happened riding a limo with an upper-class Cuban couple after a gala I had entertained at. Even though I said I was Cuban in my routine, the Cuban couple still could not believe it and asked: "You are Puerto Rican, aren't you?" They did not see the fruits, the accent, the loud behavior reflected in their own Cuban mirror.

At present Carmelita has put away her classic fruit and opted for donning camouflage, Desert Storm, and animal prints, faux snake, faux leopard, faux cow, no faux Foucault.

As a writer, I do confess to being jealous of Carmelita and, ingrate that I am, have wanted to kill that persona who has served me so well, who ironically gave me my voice, that persona who lets me see beyond the printed word. Oh, how I cried when a Boston reviewer described me as one who had horn-rimmed glasses, orange hair with black roots and buck teeth. But it was Carmelita who said buck up, girl: black roots, that's right, be proud of your African black roots; buck teeth, I say delicious overbite a la Brigitte Bardot and Patricia Arquette, and watch out cause I bite. Grrrr.

I EXIT YOU ENTER

And now, dear reader, I hope that as you turn these pages, you'll find that the work entertains you; that the work moves you, tugging at your heartstrings; but that the work is also thought provoking and ponders universal questions like the African saying that asks: ¿Con qué culo se sienta la cucaracha? With what ass does the cockroach sit?

Plays / Performance Script

Memorias de la Revolución / Memories of the Revolution

Written by Carmelita Tropicana and Uzi Parnes
Directed by Uzi Parnes
Designed by Uzi Parnes
Lighting by Joni Wong
Staged managed by Mary Patierno
Projections by Ela Troyano
Costumes by House of Chandalier and Quinn

Memorias de la Revolución was first presented as a work in progress at WOW in 1986. In 1987 it was presented at Performance Space 122 with only one cast change: Annie Iobst replaced Holly Hughes in the roles of Brendah/Tropicanette.

Cast

Carmelita Tropicana/Pingalito Betancourt: herself
Brendah/Tropicanette: Annie Iobst
Brendaa/Tropicanette: Alison Rooney
Machito/Tropicanette: Maureen Angelos
Capitán Maldito/Tropicanette: Kate Stafford
Marimacha/Tropicanette: Peggy Healey
Juanita/El Tuerto/Go-Go Dancer: Quinn
Rosita Charo Rosita Charo/Tropicanette: Lisa Kron
Lota Hari/Nota: Diane Jeep Ries
The Virgin on Film: Uzi Parnes

Act I: Havana, 1955
Act II: Lost at sea in a rowboat, 1955
Act III: New York City, 1967

PROLOGUE

On stage is a screen with a projected slide of a tourist postcard of Havana circa 1940. The word *Havana* is boldly written on it. Carmelita Tropicana enters. She holds a rose in her hand.

CARMELITA

Memories from the deep recess cavity of my mind, misty water color. . . . Memorias—we all have them. (To audience) You do. And I, Carmelita Tropicana, have them of my beloved country Cuba. (Looking back at the slide projection) Who knew in 1955 what was to happen to us? Who knew then what destiny was to be? If maybe my baby brother Machito had his mind more on the revolution and his date with destiny than on his date with the two Americanas, who knows? Who knows?

She flings the rose at the audience and exits. Blackout.

ACT I

Scene 1

On the screen is a slide projection of the capitol building in Havana. Two American tourists, Brendah and Brendaa, dressed in similar polka-dot dresses, enter and stand in front of the slide. They are waiting.

BRENDAA

Oh Brendah, I can't believe we are actually in Havana—love capital of the world. Everything is so romantic. (Looking in dictionary) Albondigas.

BRENDAH

Albóndigas. (Looking in dictionary) Meatballs.

BRENDAA

I never knew Latin men could be so—

BRENDAH

Sexy, virile, gay caballeros.

BRENDAA

Yes, but so sweet and gentle. Machito would never hurt a mosquito.

BRENDAH

Well, I saw him first. I'm more his type.

BRENDAA

Says who?

BRENDAH

I say.

BRENDAA

Well, we'll just have to see when he gets here.

BRENDAH

What time is it? He should be here by now.

BRENDAA

Brendah, in the tropics everything is slow. Maybe he overdid his siesta.

Blackout.

Scene 2

Lights up on Carmelita waiting in front of a slide of a Havana street with a flower cart. She is pacing anxiously. She is wearing dark sunglasses and is writing in a little notebook.

CARMELITA

Ai, Dios mío, Machito.

Machito enters. He has a beard and sunglasses and is selling peanuts.

MACHITO

Maní, maní. Peanuts, señorita?

CARMELITA

Beat it, I'm busy.

MACHITO

Señorita, don't you want to buy some peanuts (removing beard) from that handsome brother you got?

CARMELITA

(Hitting him) Machito, idiota. I kill you. I wait here an hour for you. This is dangerous. He's going to pass by any minute now.

MACHITO

I'm sorry, I didn't know.

CARMELITA

Never mind. The money.

MACHITO

Here. Minus three dollars for the beard and peanuts.

CARMELITA

Here are the papers. Now listen. I've been trailing him for a month. It's always the same, like clockwork. At eight o'clock El Tuerto picks him up at the house and they drive here to that store to get his shoes shined and pick up a newspaper. At nine he is at the police station. At nine-ten he goes to the bathroom and by nine-twenty he is ready to torture. He eats at one and at two El Tuerto brings him a woman from Casa Marina. He likes that brothel the best. It's where the U.S. Navy goes.

Machito gets really excited.

CARMELITA

Can you believe it, Machito? On the door it's got a sign with a little American flag saying: "American Surgeon General Seal of Approval." On the door. What do they think this is, part of the Good Neighbor Policy?

MACHITO

(Aroused) Every day a different woman?

CARMELITA

Yes, disgusting but quick. At two-thirty he is snoring. By three-thirty he is back to torturing until he leaves at six o'clock. It takes him an hour to get home because he stops to snack along the way: frog legs, oysters, flan. At seven he is home. Between seven and seven-thirty he is home. That's when you strike.

MACHITO

Between seven and seven-thirty.

CARMELITA

Then meet me at the Malecón. Quick, Machito, I think that is his car. Go that way.

Machito exits. Carmelita waits, looks around, and exits also.

Scene 3

Slide changes back to the capitol building where Brendah and Brendaa are waiting. They are pacing.

BRENDAH

He must have been bitten by a some tsetse fly. He's more than an hour late.

BRENDAA

Oh there he is.

BRENDAH

Hola, you tamale.

BRENDAA

¿Cómo estás, macho?

BRENDAH

Hola, muchachas.

BRENDAA

¿Cuándo begins el tour grande?

MACHITO

I'm very busy today. I can't go on tour, but here are two tickets to Tropicana, the hot nightclub of Havana. You get in free. I meet you there tonight, okay?

BRENDAH

But I got all dressed up for the cigar factory.

BRENDAA

I got my bikini underneath. (Seductively) Muchas polka dotas.

BRENDAH

(Grabbing him by his tie) You promised.

BRENDAA

We paid in advance.

MACHITO

Okay. We do quick tour.

The slides in the background change as Machito names different tourist spots and they all run in place.

MACHITO

This is the capitol building.

BRENDAH

I know. We've been standing here for an hour.

MACHITO

El Morro Castle.

BRENDAH

Can we go in?

MACHITO

No. No. This is the statue of Maceo.

BRENDAA

I can't run in these heels.

MACHITO

The arch of . . .

BRENDAA

Weren't we here before?

MACHITO

You Americanas you crackers me up. This is the beach. Well, I gotta go. See you in Tropicana.

BRENDAH

That was some fast tour. I know this island is small, but this is ridiculous.

BRENDAA

I told you we should have gone to the Dominican Republic.

Blackout.

Scene 4

Later that night. The slide changes to the outside of Capitán Maldito's house. Slide changes once again to a window. In the darkness, Machito and his cohort, Marimacha, carry music cases which actually contain machine guns they will use to assassinate Capitán Maldito.

MARICHAMA

(Taking a kung fu stance) I don't like it.

MACHITO

What do you mean?

MARIMACHA

It's too much like an American gangster movie—dressing up like musicians.

MACHITO

Shh. Listen.

They get closer to the house and peer through the window. They hear lovemaking noises.

WOMAN (offstage)

Dámelo, papi. Papi dámelo. Dámelo.

MACHITO

Pig. Let's go.

They shoot their machine guns. A woman screams. Dogs bark.

MACHITO

Oh shit. That's not Maldito. Marimacha, run. Where's Pepe with the car?

They exit. Car screeching sounds are heard.

Scene 5

Later that night. Inside a bus crowded with passengers, including Brendah and Brendaa. Pingalito, the conductor of the bus, is taking money when Machito, wearing a kerchief over his mouth and nose, jumps into the bus and holds a gun to Pingalito.

MACHITO

(To Pingalito) Do you believe in Cuba?

PINGALITO

The country or the singer?

MACHITO

Don't be a wise guy.

BRENDAH

¿Cuánto dinero, señor?

BRENDAA

¿Dónde está el Malecón?

MACHITO

Tell them to—

PASSENGER 1

Hey, this is my stop.

PASSENGER 2

Thief, ladrón!

MACHITO

Tell them to be quiet or else.

PINGALITO

Mi gente, relax. I'm ok. You're ok.

MACHITO

I have a little time and so do you. Have you ever been to Tropicana?

The passengers, who have been eavesdropping, repeat Tropicana, one at a time.

MACHITO

My sister Carmelita is the manager there. You let me be the conductor on this bus tonight and I will spare you your life and let you into Tropicana for free. If not, you'll die; but worse, Cuba will not be free. She will suffer. Go take this message to Carmelita: The banana was not sliced. Do you understand?

PINGALITO

The banana was not sliced.

MACHITO

Gracias, hermano. Brother, we will win.

BRENDAA

Oh, they're brothers.

Blackout.

Scene 6

Later that night at the Tropicana nightclub. There is a red-orange lamé curtain with lime-green ruffles. A cigarette girl enters and tries to sell cigarettes to the audience. Rosita Charo Rosita Charo sticks her head out and signals to the cigarettte girl to beat it. The show is about to begin.

ROSITA

(Pointing out that the dress she is wearing is made of the same fabric as the curtain)

Bienvenidos, damas y caballeros. Yo soy Rosita Charo Rosita Charo. Bienvenidos a Tropicana. Welcome, ladies and gentlemen, to the most fabulous club in the world: Tropicana. Presentamos hoy. We present for you today the Tropicanettes' salute to our neighbors in El Norte: the United States.

The curtain opens to reveal a platform stage with two cabaret tables. In the background there is an Henri Rousseau backdrop with lots of palm trees and flowers. The Tropicanettes are posed in front of it. Rosita joins them in the song "Yes, We Have No Bananas." The Tropicanettes have large fruits attached to their costumes on their rears.

Yes, We Have No Bananas

There's a grocer on our street
It's run by a spic
And she gives good things to eat
But you should hear her speak
When you ask her anything
She never answers no.
She just yeses you to death
And as she takes your dough
She tells you
Yes, we have no bananas
We have no bananas today.

There's peaches and berries
Pineapples and cherries
And all kinds of fruit I'd say
We have an old-fashioned tomato
Long Island potato

But yes, we have no bananas
We have no bananas today.
No tenemos no bananas aquí.
Hay tacos, burritos, frijoles con chile
And all kinds of things are crazy
But we have some old-fashioned tortillas
Long Island tequila
But yes we have no bananas
No tenemos no bananas aquí.

When the song ends and the Tropicanettes take their final pose, Pingalito comes out and sings "The banana was not sliced." As the curtain closes he stands in front of it and delivers his monologue to the audience.

PINGALITO

Life is strange. One day you go to your job, you punch tickets, and the next day the tide of history has swept you out to sea and you have to sink or swim with the sharks. "The banana was not sliced." Code words for attempted assassination of Capitán Maldito, Havana's chief of police and most feared man in all of Cuba. Bienvenidos, damas y caballeros, al show du jour *Memorias de La Revolución*, the personal memoirs of the daughter of the Cuban Revolution, star of stage and screen, Carmelita Tropicana. This revolution you witness here tonight happened in 1955 in Havana, but you do not find it yet in the history books. This is why Carmelita calls me, Pingalito Betancourt, in Miami, to come here and present multimedia extravaganza.

You see, I was the conductor of the M15 bus route that go from La Habana Vieja to El Vedado. Let me explain. (Scratching his crotch while talking) In Cuba, there were two people on the bus—the bus driver, the muscle of the operation, and the conductor. The brains, the financial advisor, in short, I Pingalito, I am the Socrates of the M15 bus route. The first time Carmelita gets on my bus and I smell the Heaven Scent perfume, what can I do? I forget my job as financial advisor and let her in for free. When I remember that day, ladies and gentlemen—los pelos se me paran de punta. My hairs stand on end. In that tight red dress, Carmelita was the symbol of Cuban womanhood. Like Carmelita, Havana in 1955 was very gay like the music: mambo, rumba, y cha cha cha. But underneath the political climate was turbulent, churning, growling like the starving stomach of a 500-pound football player. In order for you to enjoy the show tonight, I will give you my own perspective of Cuba—from history, geography, and culture. As a matter of fact, I have in my possession a document. (He takes out a placemat with a map of Cuba and facts about Cuba.) Audiovisual aid number one, this placemat I pick up in Las Lilas restaurant of Miami, titled "Facts about Cuba." As you can see the island of Cuba is shaped like a Hoover vacuum cleaner with Pinar del Río as the handle. How many of you know fact one? Cuba is known as the pearl of the Antilles because of its natural wealth and beauty. And the first thing we learn as little children is that when Christopher Columbus landed in our island, kneeling down he said: "Esta es la tierra más hermosa que ojos humanos han visto." This is the most beautiful land that human eyes have seen. The beaches of Varadero, the majestic mountains of La Sierra Maestra. But, ladies and gentlemen, nothing can compare with the beauty of the human landscape. Oye, mi hermano, those chorus girls of Tropicana with the big breasts, thick legs. In Cuba we call girls carros, but I mean your big old American cars like Cadillac, no Nissan or Toyota. Like the Dancer Tongolele. I swear to you or my name is not Pingalito Betancourt. You could put a tray of daiquirís on Tongolele's behind and she could walk across the floor without spilling a single drop. That, ladies and gentlemen, is landscape. Give me a gun and I fight for that landscape.

Fact two. Cuba is 759 miles long and is smaller than Pennsylvania. Wait a second, I got a cousin in Pennsylvania. I see, Springmaid. This is written by Americans. Mi gente, don't believe everything you read. Let's see if fact three is correct.

Fact three. Spanish is the official language of Cuba. This is true. It's a beautiful language. You talk with your hands, with your mouth. There is an interesting expression in Cuba when you want to find out the color of someone. You say. Oye mi hermano, Y tu abuela ¿dónde está? Tell me brother, where is your grandmother?

This brings us to fact four. Three-fourths of all Cubans are white of Spanish descent. And a lot of these three fourths have a very dark suntan all year round. It reminds me of a story my grandmother told me about a fancy restaurant run by a woman from Spain, Doña Pilar. One day, a black couple comes to the restaurant to eat. They are very well dressed. It is the first time a black couple comes to the restaurant to eat. Doña Pilar serves them very polite. But when they leave, what do you think Doña Pilar do with all they dishes they ate from? She takes every plate and in front of the customers she smashes them.

When they ask me, Pingalito where is your grandmother? I say mulata y a mucha honra. Dark and proud.

Fact five. The name Cuba comes from the Indian word Cubanacan meaning "center place." Because we Cubans know we are the center of the universe. In Cuba there is a saying: No quedó ni un indio para contar su historia. There was not one Indian left to tell his story, because the Spanish conquistadores killed them all. But Cuba did not forget her Indians, no. She names her ice cream after the beautiful Indian Guarina, better than Haagen Daz. She names her national beverage after the Indian Hatuey—malta Hatuey. And the great composer, el maestro Lecuona, honors that Cuban Indian Siboney. Ladies and gentlemen, I think you now know all there is to know about Cuba, so let us relive those memories with a tribute to that great Cuban Indian, Siboney.

Curtain opens once again for "Siboney," a song-and-dance number. While Rosita and Marimacha sing the song on one side of the stage, a story is re-enacted through dance. Two Indian maidens with bow and arrow appear from the opposite side of the stage and dance. Siboney, the Indian chief, is standing in the middle of the stage as they dance around him. A white hunter with a shotgun comes out during the song, takes aim at Siboney, and shoots him. Siboney falls, the white hunter exits, and the two Indian maidens go and revive Siboney, who holds both as the song ends.

Siboney

Siboney, si tú no me quieres voy a morir
Siboney, yo te quiero, yo me muero por tu amor.
Siboney, tu boca la más hermosa su dulzor
Ven aquí que te quiero
Y todo tesoro eres tú para mí.
Siboney al arrullo
De tu palma pienso en tí.
Siboney, de mis sueños
Si no oyes la de mi voz.
Ai, Siboney, si no vienes
Me moriré de amor,
Me moriré de dolor.
Siboney de mis sueños
Te espero con ansia en mi carey.
Oh, Siboney
Porque tú eres el dueño
De mi amor, Siboney
Oye lejos de mi canto de cristal.

No te pierdas por el mundo
Mar igual.

At the end of the song Marimacha kisses Rosita's hand. Rosita exits. Machito comes in and sits at the table and Marimacha joins him.

MACHITO

Dos Cuba libres, Juanita.

MARIMACHA

The night is still young. We will try again. You scared?

MACHITO

Me, Machito, scared? Jamás. (Gulping down drink) It's in my blood. This time, Marimacha, we do it right. We don't make the same mistake. We get Capitán Maldito or my name is not Machito.

I'll never forget, when I was four years old, my papa calls me to his room. He say, "Machito, come over here and stop playing with the cucarachas." I was a kid, what did I know? To me they were my friends. I made them a little house. "Ven acá," Papa said. "You Machito, you are hombrecito now, little man." He says he has to go away soon. He goes to the drawer and takes out a pistol and bullets and puts them in my little hand. "From now on, Machito, you will protect your mama and sisters: Carlota, Carmita, Cachita, Carmelita, Conchita, Cukita, y Baba." That night I hear whispers. I see papa tearing up photographs. Mama puts me to bed. In the middle of the night, I hear a knock on the door, heavy footsteps on the stairs, I hear my mama cry. They take my papa away, that Capitán Maldito and his man El Tuerto, the one-eyed. I swear on that day revenge. Venceremos. Brother, we will win.

They toast and a flurry of gunshots are heard. They hide under the table. After the shooting is over, they come up.

MARIMACHA

It's begun—stage one of Operation Fry the Banana.

MACHITO

Maduro or tostones?

MARIMACHA

Maduro, of course. Sweet fried bananas taste better with beans.

MACHITO

Full steam ahead like a locomotive. There's no going back. Maldito will squeal like a pig. (Squealing) Dead pig. You and me, Marimacha, we've been through a lot.

MARIMACHA

Remember our first time with Bibi and Beba.

MACHITO

The twins with the cute little mustaches. And their father. The big shot engineer. Thinks we are not good enough. Low life chusma. Asking us which beach club we belong to. (Imitating a snob) "We belong to the Havana Yacht Club." The high class, high life makes me sick.

MARIMACHA

Well, we fix him good.

MACHITO

I would have loved to have seen his face when we knocked off the power generator in his plant. Ha. The big cheese gotta go to the office, we little cheeses run off with the twins.

MARIMACHA

(Toasting) ¡Viva Bibi!

MACHITO

¡Viva Beba! (Melancholically) Juventud, divino tesoro.

MARIMACHA

You are right. Youth is a fine treasure. We are still young. (Trying to coax him out of his mood) Machito, think of the future. History will remember us, our revolution, our art. (Pointing to herself) Who is the Cuban Bing Crosby? Who is the Emily Dickinson?

MACHITO

You are right. You know, I went out with an American girl once. Jane Hayes. Blond eyes, blue hair. American girls don't take showers every day like us.

MARIMACHA

I know.

MACHITO

She didn't wear a brassiere.

MARIMACHA

Yeah. American girls are loose. Not like our Cuban flores.

MACHITO

What time is it? Carmelita should be here by now.

A flurry of gunshots is heard and they duck under the table as Brendah and Brendaa enter.

BRENDAH

Are you sure this the Tropicana? It doesn't look like much of a hot spot.

BRENDAA

The sign outside said Troiana. The *p* and the *c* were missing.

They sit at the table where Marimacha and Machito are hiding.

MARIMACHA

Machito, looks like this table has more legs.

MACHITO

My little turistas Americanas.

BRENDAA & BRENDAH

Machito!

MACHITO

Brendah and Brendaa, I like you to meet my friend, Marimacha.

BRENDAA

Mucho gusto, señor. (To Brendah) I'm beginning to speak like a native.

BRENDAH

Machito, can you order me something to wet my whistle?

MACHITO

Whistle?

BRENDAH

Drink, tomar.

MACHITO

Oh, sí, drink.

BRENDAA

Do you have any blender drinks?

MARIMACHA

We have Cuba libre. (Yelling) It means free Cuba. Cuban rum and American Coca-Cola. Very good. You like it.

BRENDAA

Your name is Mary macha?

MARIMACHA

Marimacha. I am a singer. (Singing.)

BRENDAH

I love a serenade. I see you're not doing so bad yourself.

BRENDAA

Oh, Brendaa (pointing to her ring finger). Maybe we leave Havana with a big rock.

BRENDAH

Machito, maybe you need a private secretary to take dictation.

Another flurry of gunshots are heard and Machito and Marimacha get under the table.

BRENDAA

Are those fireworks?

BRENDAH

What happened to our gay caballeros?

Machito and Marimacha raise the tablecloth as they speak.

MACHITO

Operation Fry the Banana. Carmelita should be here by now. Dios mío, Marimacha. I get confused. I thought I had to meet Carmelita at Tropicana but it was the Americanas at the Tropicana, and Carmelita at the Malecón. Oh, she'll kill me this time, with her temper. Don't tell her about the Americanas, okay? (To Brendah and Brendaa) Bye.

BRENDAA

That man of yours is always leaving. At least mine is still here. (They look at each other and make a dash for Marimacha who is under the table. There are cries of delight and then surprise.)

BRENDAH

Oh, Marimacha.

BRENDAA

Oh, Marimacha.

BRENDAH

Oh, Marimacha!

BRENDAA

The banana has been sliced.

BRENDAH

Oh my God, it's a she.

BRENDAA

I'll never be able to have children.

They get out from under the table and sit on the chairs. Lota Hari, wearing a seductive dress, enters and takes out a little notebook and pen and begins to write. She sits at another table. Capitán Maldito, in a white tuxedo, enters and is followed by El Tuerto, a policeman with a patch over his eye, holding a machine gun. El Tuerto goes to the table where Lota is sitting and menacingly points the gun at her.

EL TUERTO

Arriba las manos.

MALDITO

Relax, Tuerto. Let's see if we can catch a couple of bees with a little honey.

EL TUERTO

Si, mi capitán.

MALDITO

Come check out this table. (They go to the table where Brendah and Brendaa are sitting.)

BRENDAA

This must be the bad element they warned us about.

BRENDAH

They can't do anything to us. We are American citizens.

MALDITO

Americanas, of course. Skinny, flat chested. Passport.

BRENDAA

Somos Americanas, señor.

EL TUERTO

Your name.

BRENDAH

Brendah.

EL TUERTO

Your name.

BRENDAH

Brendaa.

EL TUERTO

Twins, mi capitán.

MALDITO

Don't believe everything you see.

BRENDAH

I'll say.

MALDITO

Tuerto, the test.

EL TUERTO

(Taking out a piece of paper) Who won the World Series in 1951?

BRENDAA

Yankees.

EL TUERTO

Correct.

BRENDAH

Maybe we'll win something.

EL TUERTO

What do you put on your hot dog? Is a trick question.

Brendah and Brendaa confer.

BRENDAA

Mustard.

EL TUERTO

Wrong. Sauerkraut. I told you it was a trick. What is the name of your President Eisenhower's dog?

BRENDAH

Muffy.

EL TUERTO

Correct.

MALDITO

Two out of three. Not bad. Tuerto, go check out the back. See if we have a couple of worms hiding.

EL TUERTO

A sus órdenes, mi capitán. (He exits. Maldito goes to sit at the table with Brendah and Brendaa and snaps a finger at Marimacha.)

MALDITO

You want five to life, or you want to pull up a chair for an illustrious gentleman like myself? (Marimacha pulls out the chair.) That's what I like, fast service. A man knows quality when he sees it. Quality likes quality. Recognizes itself. That's why I smoke tabacos Partagas. Cuba, cigar capital of the world. They take years to make. Lots of Negroes in the field singing. Singing and rolling. Ai, mamá Inés, ai mamá Inés, todos los negros tomamos café. I'm like the sweet jerez of Spain. But I guess you American girls can tell that just by looking at me. I bet you are here, like all the Americanas we get, to look for the real thing. Un macho who will make you feel like a real woman. A macho like me. I am El Macho de Machos. A macho among machos. I have two cocks. One's named Adolph, for Hitler, and the other Rudolf, for the reindeer. I've got them the best equipment, custom-made German stirrups. Ah, there's nothing like a cockfight. But don't go wearing white. Always wear red. You can say I always had an affinity for poultry. My grandfather used to take me to the market place. The chickens would be cackling. My grandpa taught me responsibility. He'd say, "Which one?" And I got to finger the chicken I wanted. The Chinaman in the market would grab the chicken I chose. (He demonstrates, grabbing Brendaa by the neck.) With his left hand, and with his right the ax. He would lay the head on the block and whack. The head would roll. Minutes later, the body would be shaking in a cha cha cha. That's the macho way. I never liked my grandmother's way. With a sharp knife she would cut the jugular vein until it bled to death. The head would go in circles and finally die like Alicia Alonso in *Swan Lake*. I don't like ballet. Faggot stuff. I like real entertainment. I hear there's a singer I used to know here tonight. (Yelling) Isn't that right, Rosita?

ROSITA

Offstage. (Disguising her voice) Rosita went home.

MALDITO

You don't fool me Rosita Charo Rosita.

ROSITA

I can't, I'm busy.

MALDITO

You want El Tuerto to come get you?

ROSITA

No, not that.

BRENDAH

Maybe it's time we banana split. (They try to sneak out, but Maldito restrains them.)

MALDITO

You Americanas will stay to hear Rosita sing. Come on Rosita. (He grabs her forcefully.) Show them some real singing.

ROSITA

No, Maldito.

MALDITO

What did you say?

ROSITA

Tropicanettes, the banana number.

MALDITO

No, banana number. Our song.

ROSITA

No, Maldito, not in front of . . .

MALDITO

Sing it to me while we dance.

ROSITA

Please, not here.

MALDITO

Enough fooling around, Rosita. Now.

While Rosita sings "Bésame Mucho," a romantic ballad, Maldito brutally dances with her, throwing her around the stage, twisting her arms, pulling her hair, bending her fingers, and finally dropping her on the floor.

Bésame Mucho

Bésame, bésame mucho
Como si fuera esta noche la última vez

Bésame, bésame mucho.
Que tengo miedo, perderte, perderte otra vez.
Quiero tenerte muy cerca
Mirarme en tus ojos
Verte junto a mí
Pienso que tal vez mañana
Yo estaré muy lejos, muy lejos de tí.

MALDITO

(Grabbing her by the hair, he throws her on the table where Brendah and Brendaa are sitting.) Translation for our American friends.

ROSITA

Kiss me, kiss me a lot.
I'm afraid of losing you again.
I want to have you near me
To look at myself in your eyes
See you next to me.
I think that maybe tomorrow
I'll be far away from you.
If you should leave me
Each little dream would take me
A lie would be true

Bésame, bésame mucho
Love me, love me forever and make
All my dreams come true.

Rosita sobs as Maldito drops her on the floor.

MALDITO

That was touching, Rosita. I couldn't have sung it more beautiful myself.

El Tuerto comes in with Machito, who is handcuffed. El Tuerto throws Machito on his knees.

EL TUERTO

Look at the worm I found in the alleyway, mi capitán.

MALDITO

Good work, Tuerto. Machito Tropicana: bad poet, bad revolutionary. You look like your father Camacho, only more stupid. You try to kill me twice, first you kill my dog Buster. Then you kill my wife. I get big fat insurance. We are going to hear mucho from you tonight down at police headquarters. It is going to be pretty poetry. Ha. Not like this. (Reading from matchbook) The police found this in my house. Read it, Tuerto.

EL TUERTO

My beautiful Brendah y Brendaa,
My heart to you I will, I will . . .

He goes to the Americanas to figure out the word, and as he does, Marimacha, who is at the table, grabs a bottle and smashes it over his head. El Tuerto slumps over the table, dazed. Maldito takes out his gun, shoots, and Marimacha and Machito run out. El Tuerto and Maldito run after Marimacha and Machito, and exit.

During the fight and shooting, both Brendah and Brendaa are oblivious to the action, instead fighting with one another over who will get the matchbook with Machito's love poem.

BRENDAH

Beautiful Brendah y Brendaa

BRENDAA

My heart to you I will surrendah

BRENDAH

Embrace Machito, great poet of Havana.

BRENDAA

Oh, skinny and loose Americanas. (Happily) That's us.

BRENDAH

Let's rumba tonight at Tropicana.

BRENDAA

My heart to you I will surrendah. It's beautiful.

BRENDAH

Latin men are so sensitive.

Rosita is lying on the floor sobbing when Carmelita enters.

BRENDAA

There she is. I saw her picture outside. That's Carmelita Tropicana.

ROSITA

(Sobbing more hysterically now) Oh, Carmelita . . .

CARMELITA

(To Rosita) What happened?

(Rosita continues to sob and Carmelita finally slaps her. While Rosita and Carmelita are engaged, Brendah and Brendaa are stealing ashtrays and whatever else they can get their hands on as souvenirs from the club.)

ROSITA

Thank you, Carmelita. It was awful. Maldito came.

CARMELITA

Machito didn't get Maldito again.

ROSITA

No. The pig makes me sing "Bésame" and El Tuerto comes and he finds Machito and it's bad, he's kneeling and the matchbook . . .

CARMELITA

What happened to Machito? Dios mío. Tell me, Rosita.

ROSITA

They shoot and Machito and Marimacha run fast. It was awful.

CARMELITA

Gracias a Dios Marimacha is with Machito. She protects him. But this is bad, Rosita. Very bad. You have to go home now and tell the Tropicanettes to go home also. I have very important urgent business tonight. (They hug.)

ROSITA

Save us, Carmelita.

CARMELITA

I try. (She goes over to the table where the Americanas have been sitting.) The banana is frying.

BRENDAA

I'm sorry, greasy food is not good for my complexion.

CARMELITA

The banana is frying.

BRENDAH

I ordered the plantains.

Carmelita spots Lota Hari, who is smoking a cigarette at the opposite end of the table, and goes over to her.

CARMELITA

The banana is frying.

LOTA

The wasps sweats. The bee stings.

CARMELITA

The monkey with the bell rings.

LOTA

Ding a link.

CARMELITA

(Going to the table with the Americanas) Time to go, Americanas. Tropicana is closed. You make enough trouble for my brother Machito already.

BRENDAH

Somos Americanas. You can't treat us this way.

CARMELITA

Out.

BRENDAA

What manners! Let's go, Brendaa.

BRENDAH

We paid and we didn't even get to see the floor show.

They exit. Carmelita goes to sit with Lota.

CARMELITA

Lota?

LOTA

Yah, Carmelita.

CARMELITA

Sí. ¡Viva Cuba!

LOTA

(Icy and detached) Viva.

CARMELITA

Finally you arrive. We have been waiting for you.

LOTA

(Looking at her watch) Und I have been waiting for you.

CARMELITA

A little delay. My brother Machito is a great poet, but not so good revolutionary. He forgot he gotta meet me at the Malecón.

LOTA

He is a little geshtunka.

CARMELITA

I know, geshtunka, but what can I do—he is family. Let's talk revolution.

LOTA

Let's talk business.

CARMELITA

Very well. You have the equipment and supplies?

LOTA

Yah.

CARMELITA

Two hundred machine guns, one hundred submachine guns, three hundred rifles, two thousand grenades.

LOTA

Und one tank.

CARMELITA

Loaded.

LOTA

My guns are always loaded.

CARMELITA

Twenty-five thousand dollars.

LOTA

That is correct.

CARMELITA

And ammunition?

LOTA

That is not in the contract.

CARMELITA

Maybe we change the contract a little.

LOTA

Five thousand dollars for ammunition.

CARMELITA

But, Lota we are poor.

LOTA

It's business.

CARMELITA

It's revolution.

LOTA

That is not my problem. I am a spy, a professional.

CARMELITA

Lota, people are dying; children are hungry.

LOTA

It is business. Five thousand dollars for ammunition.

CARMELITA

But Lota, what good is guns without ammunition? It's like a flower without petals, a car without wheels.

LOTA

I'm sorry.

CARMELITA

Couldn't you give the revolution a little break?

LOTA

I feel for your position, but . . .

CARMELITA

You feel?

LOTA

All right. This goes against all my principles. Four thousand dollars for the ammunitions.

CARMELITA

Four thousand dollars?

LOTA

Four thousand dollars.

CARMELITA

The hungry children . . .

LOTA

Four thousand dollars.

CARMELITA

The starving artists . . .

LOTA

Thirty-five hundred dollars and ninety-nine cents. This is the best I can do.

CARMELITA

Give me your hand. I see you are a stubborn Leo.

LOTA

Ya, Leo, nein stubborn. Sensible. How did you know this?

CARMELITA

I see many things, Lota. I am voyeur. I feel many things. This is why I am an artist revolutionary. I sing; I fight. (Looking at Lota's palm) I see you have been a spy all your life.

LOTA

That is correct.

CARMELITA

I see two women in your life.

LOTA

Ya. Meine grandmother, the great Mata Hari, and her daughter Meine Mutti Wata Hari.

CARMELITA

They used to put you to bed singing:

Men and women swoon
When they see my arms aflutter.

LOTA

They begin to stutter

CARMELITA

They call me Mata—Mata

LOTA

Mata Hari

CARMELITA

My dance is like a wild safari

LOTA

Better than a Kama

CARMELITA

Sutra Indian in a

CARMELITA AND LOTA

Sari.

LOTA

This is incredible Carmelita, you are . . .

CARMELITA

Your great grossmutter, the great Mata Hari, is a great spy, a dancer. She doesn't say business all the time like you. She has passion. She feels. She feels for everyone—for the French, the Spanish, the German, the Dutch. This is why they kill her. I see a little girl (she holds Lota's chin) trying to come out, to express herself. To feel, to be free. Like the Cuban people. Our struggle is your struggle. Freedom, Mata. Can you taste it? Like cold coconut water? Freedom from the tyranny of men like Maldito. Cowards. Little, big, fat men with prejudice, who torture, kill, and beat up women. I cannot pay you with Geld, but as a woman, a revolutionary, I can make sacrifice. Myself, Carmelita, for ammunition. Good men kill for less.

LOTA

Carmelita, I feel strange. Like this is the first time, I . . . (Lota, overcome with emotion, is about to kiss Carmelita, when Marimacha comes in and breaks the almost-kiss.)

MARIMACHA

Carmelita, quick. We have to leave. Machito has been captured with Pepe and taken to police headquarters.

Carmelita almost faints and they catch her.

MARIMACHA

You must be strong. He wants you to be strong. Maldito gave orders to come burn Tropicana. He found guns in Pepe's car and knows about us. We have to leave at once. There is a boat waiting for us at the Malecón. Pronto. (To Lota) You too, gorgeous.

CARMELITA

¡Vamos al Malecón!

ACT II

Scene 1

The action takes place a day later in the middle of the ocean on a rowboat. Carmelita has escaped with Lota and Marimacha. It is nighttime.

CARMELITA

How long have we been here, Marimacha?

MARIMACHA

Let's see. Night . . . mmm. I will say about twenty hours.

CARMELITA

We should see Key West already. We should go right, not left. Why did we listen to the German?

LOTA

I heard that. It's because Germans make the best precision instruments in the world. My instrument in the tropics is not so precise.

CARMELITA

Great, Lota.

LOTA

I'm trying to find our course due north by northwest. It takes a little time. It takes something you hot-tempered Latins don't know—how to be—quiet.

MARIMACHA

Well, when you find it, please let us know. I'm tired of rowing.

CARMELITA

I'm hungry.

MARIMACHA

I'm starving. (Marimacha remembers she has a candy bar she is hiding from them and sneakily takes a bite.)

LOTA

I also.

CARMELITA

(Seeing Marimacha chewing) Marimacha, what you got?

MARIMACHA

Nothing.

CARMELITA

Milky Way. Give us some.

They fight over the candy bar.

MARIMACHA

I was about to offer you some.

A ship's horn is heard.

MARIMACHA

Carmelita, look: the Love Boat.

LOTA

Das Liebe Boat. The Love Boat.

CARMELITA AND MARIMACHA

(Getting up and yelling) We're here. Save us. Estamos aquí.

LOTA

Sit down, both of you. They can't see us.

CARMELITA

Lota, get up and scream. Maybe they hear us.

LOTA

They can't hear us. Stop rocking the boat. We will capsize.

CARMELITA

No tienes sangre en las venas. Tienes hielo, hielo, hielo.

MARIMACHA

You are frozen, frozen, frozen.

LOTA

I heard you the first time. Sit.

CARMELITA

You don't order us no more. You hear? Enough. We row for twenty hours and for what? Nothing. Look at my hands. I'll never get to play the castanets anymore.

MARIMACHA

I didn't know you played the castanets.

CARMELITA

(Punches Marimacha) Why don't you do something good—like fish. You told me you were a fisher of women. Prove it. Catch us fish with your precision instrument.

LOTA

Very well. I will teach you both how it is done. First the hose. (She removes her stocking.) I need something to attract the fish. Earrings.

CARMELITA

No, it's the only pair I take out of Cuba. I can't.

MARIMACHA

We are starving and you're thinking of jewelry. Look over there. (She grabs the earring out of Carmelita's ear.)

CARMELITA

(Smacking her) Marimacha, how can you? You know who you talk to? Look at me. You have become an animal.

MARIMACHA

(Crying) I'm sorry Carmelita. I don't know what comes over me.

CARMELITA

(Comforting her) What happen, baby?

MARIMACHA

Remember the Maine. I lost my mother, my father, my two older brothers in a boat at sea. Ever since then I have such memories. I can't go to the beach. If I see suntan lotion, I start to shake.

CARMELITA

Come over here, Marimacha. It's okay. You are fine, Marimacha. Let it all out.

MARIMACHA

Thank you, Carmelita. I needed that.

CARMELITA

(Giving her the earring) Here, Lota, do what you have to do.

LOTA

(Attaching earring to hose) Here, Marimacha. Like this. I am sorry, Carmelita, I call you hot-tempered Latin.

CARMELITA

It's okay, Lota. You teach us how to fish. We survive. You are masterful with the hose.

LOTA

I learned to fish in the Black Sea. Black—your eyes are black. Schon.

CARMELITA

Schon?

LOTA

Beautiful. Your hair is schon. Your mouth is schon.

CARMELITA

Your nose is schon.

They are in an embrace about to kiss when Marimacha interrupts.

MARIMACHA

Help, hey, you guys. The fish. The fish. I lost the fish.

CARMELITA

I lost my earring.

LOTA

I lost my head.

The sound of a storm is heard. The waves start to get rougher.

LOTA

Sit down. We will capsize.

MARIMACHA

I see a storm ahead.

CARMELITA

Lota, where are we?

LOTA

Mein Gott in himmel. I think we are approaching the Bermuda Triangle.

MARIMACHA

The Bermuda Triangle?

LOTA

Bad currents. The most powerful ships like the Love Boat have been swallowed.

Storm sounds are heard: thunder, waves crashing.

CARMELITA

Marimacha, give me your oar.

MARIMACHA

I'm gonna die like my brother, my mother, my father. I wanted to die in the revolution. Not here. (She cries.)

LOTA

Marimacha, hold on two more minutes and it will be over. Hold onto the side of the boat.

Finally the storm subsides, and both Lota and Marimacha fall asleep. Two angels appear and open doors to a backdrop triptych with painted cherubs on either side. In the middle panel is a screen for a film projection of an apparition of the Virgin Mary on 16mm film.

VIRGIN

Carmelita, Carmelita.

CARMELITA

What is this? Am I hearing things? Marimacha, Lota, wake up.

VIRGIN

Shulum alechem vee gesyste?

CARMELITA

¿Habla español? What's going on here?

VIRGIN

Carmelita, don't worry so much. I have a tie line to you know who and I promise you a happy ending.

CARMELITA

Who are you? Here I am in the middle of the ocean and . . .

VIRGIN

I'm Mary, the Virgin. You have been chosen by the Goddess herself to be the next hottest Latin superstar, but you gotta wait a little.

CARMELITA

I always knew my destiny.

VIRGIN

But listen, there's a little problem. There is a difficult road ahead. Cuba will no longer be your home. Her revolution will not be your revolution. Yours will be an international cultural revolution.

CARMELITA

But what about my brother Machito?

VIRGIN

Hold your oars. Fate will have you meet your nemesis, Maldito, and when you do, you'll know what to do. As for that geshtunke brother of yours, you too will be reunited. Where was I? Oh, the revolution. Let it be your art. Your art is your weapon. To give dignity to Latin and Third World women: this is your struggle. If you accept, you will be gifted with eternal youth. You will always be as you are today, twenty-one.

CARMELITA

Nineteen, please.

VIRGIN

Okay, but you will suffer much. Spend years penniless and unknown until 1967.

CARMELITA

That is a lot of years, but for nineteen is okay. I accept.

VIRGIN

But listen, Carmelita, there is more. You must never, ever, ever . . .

CARMELITA

What? You are killing me.

VIRGIN

Or all the years will return, like to that nasty Dorian Gray.

CARMELITA

Never do what?

VIRGIN

Never let a man touch you. You must remain pure, like me.

CARMELITA

Never let a man touch me. Believe me, to Carmelita Tropicana Guzmán Jiménez Marquesa de Aguas Claras, that is never to be a problem. (She winks.)

The film of the Virgin ends as lights change and Carmelita sees land.

CARMELITA

Marimacha, Lota, wake up. (They wake up. Carmelita is ecstatic.) Look! It's Miami Beach!

Blackout.

ACT III

Scene 1

New York City, 1967. A local high school. Maldito, who has now lost a lot of weight, has a broom in his hand and is cleaning. He is wearing a janitor's cap and uniform.

MALDITO

Stupid high school kids. I'll put a bullet in your pinko brains. (He opens up an envelope with a letter and reads.) Dear Mr. Maldito, we regret to inform you that you have failed the 1967 Paramilitary Operative Examination. However, do not be discouraged. Our office has created positions in the Civilian Counterinsurgency Specialist Patrol, for which you may apply. To apply for the CCSP you need to supply us with intelligence information leading to the arrest of subversive civilians engaging in or promoting direct or indirect . . . hm. (A school bell rings. He puts the letter away, continues cleaning, and spots a poster on the wall for the opening of a new club called Tropicana-A-Go-Go. He examines the poster and laughs, and the laughter turns to coughing.) I think I got my ticket. (He exits.)

Scene 2

Later that night at the Tropicana-A-Go-Go which looks very much like the Tropicana in Havana: same palm trees, lamé curtain, and Rousseau-like backdrop. In addition there is a cage in the back with a dancer who dances throughout, and a counter. Machito enters. He is in a 1960s outfit including bell-bottoms and glasses. He carries a punch bowl. Rosita is at the counter.

MACHITO

Here is the punch, Rosita. And the tablets.

ROSITA

Tablets?

MACHITO

Yes, to make the punch taste good. But wait till I tell you when to give them out, okay?

ROSITA

Okay.

Brendah and Brendaa enter in 1960s mod outfits.

BRENDAA

Peace, Rosita.

ROSITA

Oh, Brendah y Brendaa. I am so happy to see you charming Americanas at the opening of the fabuloso Tropicana-A-Go-Go in Nueva York.

BRENDAA

I wouldn't have missed it for the world.

BRENDAH

The day I got my invitation I went shopping at the Luv In Boutique. How do you like it?

ROSITA

It is charming, like you. Carmelita is going to be so happy you come to the opening.

BRENDAA

It's been so many years. But you know, Rosita, in the picture in the marquee, Carmelita looks just like she did in 1955—so young.

BRENDAH

A little retouching around the eyes, perhaps.

ROSITA

No. It is true. She looks always the same. Is incredible.

BRENDAA

Brendah, maybe she goes to a different guru than we do. Could be her diet, maybe rice and beans and plátanos maduros. And speaking of plátanos, will Marimacha be attending this soiree tonight?

ROSITA

Yes, but she change a lot. Maybe you don't recognize her when she come in.

BRENDAA

Well, so have we, Rosita. It's the sixties. Brendah and I are part of the sexual revolution.

ROSITA

I been living in the Sowezera—the eighth street section of Miami. I don't know this sexual revolution you talk about.

BRENDAH

Don't tell me you never attended a C.R. group?

ROSITA

C.R.?

BRENDAA

Consciousness raising. When you talk in a group of women and you discuss women's issues and you come to terms with your sexuality.

BRENDAH

Yeah, like *Our Bodies, Ourselves.* We demand an orgasm.

ROSITA

(Embarrassed) You are still charming Americanas.

BRENDAA

I've come to terms with my sexuality. That is why I'm hoping I'll meet Marimacha again.

ROSITA

Well, she be here soon.

BRENDAH

Rosita, is this the punch?

ROSITA

Yes, and the tablets. Machito told me to give them out.

BRENDAH

We'll help you give them out. Okay? We'll take half.

ROSITA

That is very kind.

BRENDAH

I'm not taking any chance on getting stiffed again. You know how these Cubans are.

Brendah and Brendaa walk in to the dance area of the club and bump into Machito.

BRENDAH & BRENDAA

Machito!

BRENDAA

My God. This looks just like the Tropicana. I can't believe my eyes. And I haven't taken anything yet.

MACHITO

Brendah y Brendaa, welcome to the Tropicana-A-Go-Go. Is exact replica of Havana nightclub. Carmelita spared no expense. The curtains, the palm trees.

BRENDAH

Machito, what have you been up to all these years?

MACHITO

I now have the life of a Renaissance man. I write happenings. One musician plays guitar with his toes, another sits on a tuba, two girls read newspapers and pour spaghetti on their heads.

BRENDAA

With sauce?

MACHITO

Of course. For texture. And there is also my poetry. But I am stuck. Is so hard to write in another tongue. This English words. (Looking at his pad) What rhymes with twirl?

BRENDAA

Curl.

BRENDAH

Hurl.

BRENDAH & BRENDAA

Berle. Milton Berle.

MACHITO

Rain of fire, rain of fire. Swirl and twirl like Milton Berle. Groovy, let's dance.

Marimacha enters in a turban and orange jumpsuit. She goes to the counter where Rosita is.

ROSITA

Marimacha, I love your—hat.

MARIMACHA

Na mash ren go go, na mash ren go go, na mash ren go go.

ROSITA

Marimacha, are you consciousness raising?

MARIMACHA

No my consciousness is already raised. I'm on a different plane right now. When I chant my mantra, my chakra goes into a different tantra.

ROSITA

Chantra? Mantra? I live for years in Miami. Ah. This is sexual revolution. Our bodies, ourselves. I want an organ.

MARIMACHA

No, no. I am beyond the sexual revolution. That was last year.

ROSITA

You mean, no more . . . ? I can't say it.

MARIMACHA

Exactly. It's the new Marimacha.

ROSITA

Let me check your hat.

MARIMACHA

(Joining Machito and Brendah and Brendaa) Brendah y Brendaa, this is a spiritually uplifting experience for me.

BRENDAA

Likewise, I'm sure.

BRENDAH

Oh, Marimacha. I've been looking forward to this day for years.

Pingalito enters from the back of the club. He is wearing the same outfit as in Act I.

PINGALITO

Nineteen sixty-seven. It was a very good year. As you can see, the hot event of the year was the opening of the nightclub Tropicana-A-Go-Go. After Carmelita landed in Miami in 1955, she and Lota went to Germany. But in 1958, she came back to the United States, to Columbus, Ohio, to be reunited with her brother, Machito, who had just come out of jail. He was in very bad shape and needed her. In 1965, Lota Hari gave up the business of spying to become a very big Hollywood producer. That same year, Carmelita was on a plane that crashed in Nepal. Everybody thought she was . . . but in 1967, Carmelita came back and Lota was so happy, she beg Carmelita to take money for a new nightclub, Tropicana-A-Go-Go. But to go back to 1955, when Carmelita and Lota were vacationing in the Black Forest of Germany. They saw a terrible car accident. The two people in the car were dead, but out came a little blonde girl with tears in her face, crying mein Vater, meine Mutter, Dead, Dead. Lota and Carmelita adopted her and named her Carme Lota Nota Hari. Nota for short. Lota taught her spying, Carmelita singing. Let us welcome that little girl, who has blossomed into the folk singer of today, Nota Hari.

Pingalito exits. Nota Hari enters the stage with guitar in hand. She is wearing hot pants. Machito, Brendaa, Brendah, and Marimacha watch her perform.

NOTA

Before I begin my song I'd like to read a telegram from my adopted mother Lota Hari. Dear Nota and Carmelita, my body is in Hollywood, but my heart is in Tropicana-A-Go-Go tonight. Much success, signed, mother, lover, executive producer Lota. This is for you meine mutti.

Eve of Destruction

Tell me over and over again, my friend
You don't believe we're on the eve of destruction
You're old enough to kill
But not for voting.
You don't believe in war
But what's that gun you're toting?
Even the Jordan River has bodies floating
Tell me over and over again, my friend,
You don't believe we're on the eve of destruction.

Everyone claps and Nota goes to join the others. Maldito enters and stands at the counter before Rosita, who does not recognize him.

ROSITA

Check your—(smelling his cigar) Partagas. Maldito.

MALDITO

After all these years, Rosita Charo, you still have it for me? (He tries to kiss her and she fights him off.)

ROSITA

You are repulsive.

MALDITO

Playing hard to get. Rosita. So many years. I need your titties on my face.

ROSITA

You disgust me, you skinny gross pig.

MALDITO

(Grabbing her hand) It's still big. (He starts to cough.)

ROSITA

I throw up. Your lungs will come out in black heaps.

MALDITO

I'm still young. I have plans.

ROSITA

What plans?

MALDITO

I need something on Carmelita.

ROSITA

You never get anything on her. She is a saint.

MALDITO

What is this?

ROSITA

This is punch and tablets. Not for pigs.

MALDITO

(Examining the tablets) I knew it. This place is a front. Evidence.

ROSITA

(Screaming) Carmelita, Machito is the pig Maldito.

Carmelita enters the stage running. Machito lunges for Maldito, but trips on his way to him.

MACHITO

Coño.

Marimacha also lunges for Maldito.

CARMELITA

No, Machito. No, Marimacha.

MARIMACHA

(Suffering from a conflict between religious forgiveness and violence) Na mash ren go go, na mash ren go go. Pig, swine. Na mash ren . . . my hat, my beads. I want to kill the sonamambitch.

CARMELITA

No violence. It is the age of Aquarius.

NOTA

But mami, I heard about this greaseball. Let me give him one deadly karate chop.

CARMELITA

No, Nota.

MALDITO

You can't do anything to me. I am Maldito. Carmelita Tropicana, after all these years, we finally meet again. I have evidence against you. Look, tablets of drugs. I knew this place was a front for drugs and revolution. Once a revolutionary, always a revolutionary.

MARIMACHA

Once a pig, always a pig. Na mash ren go go.

MALDITO

This evidence will get me in the CCSP, of the CIA. I will be on top again.

While Maldito is speaking, Brendah shows Carmelita the tablets she is holding in her hand; Carmelita signals for Brendah to put them into the punch.

CARMELITA

Capitán Maldito. Yes. Yes. (Signaling to Brendah to put tablets in the drink) Finally we meet again. You are a better man than I am. You have beat me. The better man won.

MALDITO

CCSP, here I come.

CARMELITA

A toast.

BRENDAH

(Seductively handing Maldito a glass of punch that has been spiked) Maybe you need a secretary to help you take dictation.

MALDITO

Maybe I do. (He drinks.) Good punch. Now I give up my job as janitor in the high school. I am in command once . . . the C . . . the C is coming out of my mouth.

Maldito begins to trip as Op Art images on slides and film are projected onto the stage and on the actors.

BRENDAH

That's not all that's not all that's gonna come out of your mouth, buster.

MALDITO

Oh. Oh. Buster. (He goes to the go-go dancer in the cage and kneels in front of her.) Buster. Don't you recognize your master? (He staggers to the center of the stage and everyone surrounds him.)

CARMELITA

I, Carmelita Tropicana, in the name of all here at Tropicana-A-Go-Go, j'accuse Maldito. Let the witnesses to your crimes step forward. Marimacha, step forward.

MARIMACHA

I saw you torture for no reason, kill good people. Na mash ren go go. But when I see your face, I want to get on a tank and roll over your decrepit body.

MALDITO

Ah, tank my legs.

CARMELITA

Machito.

MACHITO

You kill my papa when I am four years old. I never learned to play beisbol with him. Two years in jail. (He lifts his shirt to show scars.) Look at my scars. Touch them.

BRENDAH

(Grabbing Maldito's hand to put on Machito's back) Feel him, touch him, heal him.

MALDITO

I didn't mean to.

CARMELITA

You didn't mean to.

ROSITA

You humiliate me. You beat me. My high heels will step all over you. (She steps on him and is overcome with emotion.)

CARMELITA

Rosita, enough. Basta. It's my turn now.

Carmelita goes into an incantation while the others do a line dance and chant the chorus of "Bongo, bongo, bongo."

CARMELITA

Maldito, if justice prevails
In hell you'll burn
But before that
Your earthly fate you can't escape.
Tonight in full you will be paid.

Oh moon of Nepal
Oh moon of Cooch Behar,
Appearing, disappearing
Playing peek-a-boo
Like Desi Arnaz
We sing to you
Babalú Babalú Aye
Oh, Gods of Africa
Yemalla y Obatala
Grant favor to your humble servant
Who speaks Shakespearean verse
And transform this flesh and spirit

To another universe.
Let my incantation
Be full of syncopation
With the heartbeat of the jungle
The drumming of the Bongo

Bongo Bongo Bongo
Bongo beats a beat
For my dancing feet
I can't stand still
Cause I got no free will
Obsessed, possessed
with the jungle beat
Everything in me shivers
my heart, my feet, my liver
My pelvis moves like Elvis
To the bongo beat.
Molecules are jumping
Bullfrogs in the night are humping
In Peoria, Illinois,
The rooster sings to you cock-a-doodle-do
In Santiago de Cuba el gallo sings to me ki-ki-ri-ki-ki
Incarnation, incantation
Alchemy divine
Ingredients like white sugar so refined
Magic potion
Containing extract of electric eel
foreskin of baboon
Human hair with pigeon droppings
a dash of pepper, a twist of lime
Help to exorcise
The evil in this big disgusting guy.

Toward the end of the incantation the chorus has surrounded Maldito, hiding him from the audience. At the end of the incantation Carmelita sprinkles glitter on him. When he gets up, he is wearing a chicken costume. He acts like a chicken.

MALDITO

Ki-ki-ri-ki-ki. Cock-a-doodle-do.

BRENDAA

Wow, Carmelita, that was great. But what was it?

CARMELITA

Brendaa, is a little trick I pick up in Nepal. Maldito always has affinity for poultry. Well, he be cackling for the rest of his life.

BRENDAH

What a happening, mind-blowing.

ROSITA

Very groovy.

CARMELITA

Rosita. Seeing Maldito today brings such sad memories, but now that he is a chicken, the good memories come back of the place we come from and never can forget. Because where you are born, that place you carry in your heart. Let us always remember que la lucha continúa and art is our weapon.

Carmelita recites part of a verse of "Guantanamera" and the others join her, singing the chorus.

Yo soy una mujer sincera	*I am sincere woman*
De donde crece la palma	*From the land of the palm trees*
Y antes de morirme quiero	*And before dying I want to give you*
Echar mis versos del alma	*My soulful poems*

Guantanamera, guajira guantanamera
Guantanamera, guajira guantanamera

Lights fade.

The End

Milk of Amnesia / Leche de Amnesia

Written and performed by Carmelita Tropicana
Direction and dramaturgy by Ela Troyano
Production design by Kukuli Velarde
Lighting by Sandra Myers

Milk of Amnesia / Leche de Amnesia was commissioned by Performance Space 122 with funds from the Joyce Mertz Gilmore Foundation, and is based on Carmelita Tropicana's 1993 trip to Cuba sponsored by the Suitcase Fund: A Project of Ideas and Means in Cross-cultural Artist Relations, an initiative created by Dance Theatre Workshop, with funding from the Rockefeller Foundation.

Stage has a minimal look. It is divided into two halves. The left is the writer's space, and is dimly lit. It has a music stand with makeup, costumes, hats. This space simulates a backstage area where the artist will change clothes, put makeup on, and read. The right side is painted white, resembling a white cube. This space is a defined performance space (the dimly lit space is the private space; the white cube, the public space). There is a mike and mike stand, and a chair that gets placed there depending on the scene.

The piece begins in darkness with a blue light bathing the chair inside the white cube, as an audiotape with the voice of the writer is heard.

Years ago when I wasn't yet American I had a green card. On my first trip abroad the customs official stamped on my papers "stateless."

When I became a citizen, I had to throw my green card into a bin along with everybody else's green cards. I didn't want to. I was born on an island. I came here when I was seven. I didn't like it here at first. Everything was so different. I had to change. Acquire a taste for peanut butter and jelly. It was hard. I liked tuna fish and jelly.

I used to play a game in bed. About remembering. I would lie awake in my bed before going to sleep and remember. I'd remember the way to my best friend's house. I'd start at the front door of my house, cross the porch. Jump off three steps onto the sidewalk. The first house on the right looked just like my house, except it had only

one balcony. The third house was great. You couldn'
den by a wall and trees and shrubs. Whenever I'd lo
shepherd sniffed me and barked me out of his turf.
ing, crossing three streets, walking two blocks until
friend's house. I did this repeatedly so I wouldn't f
member. But then one day I forgot to remember.
happened. Some time passed and I couldn't remember the third block, then the second. Now I can only walk to the third house. I've forgotten.

I had a dream when I was a kid. (Sound of footsteps running on tape) I guess because we were refugees. Me and my cousin were fugitives running away from the police. We had to escape. We were running through the streets. We saw a manhole cover and it opened up. (Sound of metal door shutting) We went down. We were in a sewer. (Sound of dripping water, echo) We were safe. But it started to get hot. Stifling hot. And as it happens in dreams, one minute my cousin was my cousin and the next she was a peanut butter and jelly sandwich. The heat was making her melt. I held her in my hands. She was oozing down. I was crying: Don't melt, Pat. Please don't melt. I woke up in a sweat. (Alarm clock rings.)

In the morning I went to school. Our Lady Queen of Martyrs. That's when it happened. In the lunchroom. I never drank my milk. I always threw it out. Except this time when I went to throw it out, the container fell and spilled on the floor. The nun came over. Looked at me and the milk. Her beady eyes screamed: You didn't drink your milk, Grade A pasteurized, homogenized, you Cuban refugee.

After that day I changed. I knew from my science class that all senses acted together. If I took off my glasses, I couldn't hear as well. Same thing happened with my taste buds. If I closed my eyes and held my breath I could suppress a lot of the flavor I didn't like. This is how I learned to drink milk. It was my resolve to embrace America as I chewed on my peanut butter and jelly sandwich and gulped down my milk. This new milk that had replaced the sweet condensed milk of Cuba. My amnesia had begun.

Pingalito, a cigar-chomping Cuban man, enters as a mambo plays. He greets the audience. He is on the cube and brightly lit.

PINGALITO

Welcome, ladies and gentlemen, to the show du jour, *Milk of Amnesia*. I am your host Pingalito Betancourt, the Cuban Antonio Banderas.

ɔse of you who are from Cuba, you may recognize my face. I was conductor in 1955 of the M15 bus route, the route that go from La abana Vieja to El Vedado. And it was in that bus that I meet Carmelita. For Stanley Kowalski there is *A Streetcar Named Desire*. For Pingalto this was Destiny on the M15 bus route.

When I heard of Carmelita's tragic accident I rush right over, hoping a familiar face can trigger something in the deep recessed cavities of her cerebro, cerebellum, and medulla oblongata. You see, people, the doctors have their methodologies for curing amnesia, and I have mine.

I make my way through the hospital corridors saying hello to all the nice Filipino nurses and I enter her room. She is asleep, looking like an angel, mouth open, pillow wet, making puttering sounds of a car engine. And I think of a childhood memory she used to tell me about. Her grandfather who smoke a cigar would take her for a drive in his Chevrolet driving with a foot on the brake, stopping and starting, stopping and starting, stopping and starting. She would get so carsick. So I decide to simulate this memory. By blowing smoke in her face, playing with the controls of the hospital bed, making the legs go up, the head go down, up and down, up and down. I am playing her like a big accordion when a doctor comes in and says I gotta go. Something about my cigar and an oxygen tank.

But I don't give up. I return the next day. I think what, above all, is Carmelita? I tell you. Cuban. One hundred fifty percent. So I decide to tell her some facts about Cuba. See if it jiggles something. (Showing audience a map of Cuba) I have here audiovisual aid number one, a placemat I pick up in Las Lilas restaurant of Miami titled "Facts about Cuba." Ladies and gentlemen, upon further examination of this placemat, you can see that the island of Cuba is shaped like a Hoover vacuum cleaner with Pinar del Río as the handle. How many of you know Cuba is known as the "pearl of the Antilles" because of its natural wealth and beauty? And the first thing we learn as little children is that when Christopher Columbus landed in our island, kneeling down, he said: "Ésta es la tierra más hermosa que ojos humanos han visto." This is the most beautiful land that human eyes have seen. The majestic mountains of la Sierra Maestra. Our mountains, not too tall. We don't need high. If we get high we get snow, then we gotta buy winter coat. And the beaches of Varadero! But ladies and gentlemen, none can compare with the beauty of the human landscape. Óyeme 'mano. Esas coristas de Tropicana. With the big breasts, thick legs. In Cuba we call girls carros and we mean your big American cars. Your Cadillac, no Toyota or Honda. Like the dancer Tongolele. I swear to you people, or my name is not Pingalito Betancourt, you could put a tray of daiquirís on Tongolele's behind and she could walk across the floor without spilling a single drop. That, ladies and gentlemen, is landscape. For that you give me a gun and I fight for that landscape. Not oil. You gotta have priorities.

Fact two. Spanish is the official language of Cuba and it's a beautiful language. You talk with your hands, you talk with your mouth. My favorite expression when you want to find out the color of someone you say: "Óyeme 'mano ¿y tu abuela dónde está?" Tell me brother, where is your grandmother? Which brings us to fact three.

Three-fourths of all Cubans are white, of Spanish descent, and a lot of these three-fourths have a very dark suntan all year round. When they ask me, "Pingalito, and where is your grandmother?" I say, "Mulata y a mucha honra." Dark and proud.

Well, I look at Carmelita and she is not blinking and I have fifteen more facts to go. So I decide to change my route. If the M15 bus doesn't take you there maybe the M21 does. So I ask you people, what is Carmelita above all? Eh? Above all she is an artist. One hundred fifty percent. So maybe a song and a poem will do the trick. Poetry is something we Cubans have in our souls. It is our tradition. I don't know how many of you know that our liberator Jose Martí, our George Washington, is also the Emily Dickinson of Cuba. So I recite for Carmelita and for you today "Ode to the Cuban Man."

Spielberg forget your Assic Park
Some say the Cuban man is disappearing
Like the dinosaur
I say que no
The Cuban man
This specimen
Will never go away
We are here to stay

Like the Cuban crocodile
One of a kind in genus and species
You find us in the Bronx Zoo
The swamps of Zapata
Calm in the water but also volatile
So don't bother the crocodile
Because we got big mouths

We open up and swallow a horse and a cow
That's why we have the Cuban expression
Te la comiste mi hermano
You ate it bro'

The Cuban man is persistent, stubborn
Like the mosquito, always buzzing around
Why you think yellow fever was so popular

The Cuban man is the apple in his mother's eye
Even when he is a little dim of wit
To his mami he is still the favorite
And at eighty she calls him baby

The Cuban man has no spare parts
Nature did not create any excess waste
She made him compact
Not tall in height, but what street smarts
Suave, sharp, slippery, and sly
Like yuca enchumba in mojo greasy pig lard
Or like the Yankee from New England say
Slicker than deer guts on a doorknob
The Cuban man has a head for business
He combines the Jewish bubbullah with the African babalú
And that's why they call him the Caribbean Jew

Above all the Cuban man is sensitive, sentimental, simpaticón
With sex appeal for days
And this is where our problem comes
It is our hubris, our Achilles' tendón
It is our passionate and romantic side
We love women too much
Too many women, too many kids

But when you tally up
The good, the bad
You too will decide
He is like a fine Havana cigar
The one you gotta have
After a big heavy meal with an after-dinner drink and

Coffee on the side
Because he is the one that truly, truly satisfies

Pingalito exits the white cube as the audiotape with the writer delivering the following monologue comes on. While tape plays, the actress takes off Pingalito's costume revealing white shorts and white T-shirt, which will be Carmelita's costume.

In high school I was asked to write an essay on the American character. I thought of fruits. Americans were apples, healthy, neat, easy to eat, not too sweet, not too juicy. Cubans were mangoes, juicy, real sweet, but messy. You had to wash your hands and face and do a lot of flossing. I stood in front of a mirror and thought I should be more like an apple. A shadow appeared and whispered: Mango stains never come off.

I didn't write about fruits in my essay. I didn't want them thinking I wasn't normal.

In the eighties, that's when my amnesia started to show cracks. As I joined the ranks of Tchaikovsky and Quentin Crisp—I became a civil servant and a thespian on the side.

As a teen I had gone to the Circle in the Square Theatre but my thespianism had been squelched the day the teacher announced the Puerto Rican Traveling Co. was holding auditions and needed actors. When she said the Puerto Rican Traveling Company everyone started to laugh. As if it was a joke. Like a Polish joke only a Puerto Rican one. I was the same as a Puerto Rican. Maybe the island was bigger, but same difference. I guessed I wouldn't do theatre.

Until I came to the WOW theatre and got cast in Holly Hughes's *The Well of Horniness*. We were asked to do it on the radio. I had a dilemma. Would my career as a civil servant be stymied if people knew I was the one who screamed every time the word *horniness* was mentioned, or that I was playing Georgette, Vicky's lover, or Al Dente, Chief of Police? Maybe I needed a new name.

As if by accident, the pieces were falling into place when I entered the WOW theatre and a comedy workshop was to take place. The teacher would not give it unless four people took it. There were three signed up for it, and with me the body count would be four. I said no. No. No. But the teacher, she was cute. So I took it.

But it wasn't me. I couldn't stand in front of an audience, wear sequined gowns, tell jokes. But she could. She who pencilled in her beauty mark, she who was baptized in the fountain of America's most popular orange juice, in the name of Havana's legendary nightclub, the Tropicana, she could. She was a fruit and wasn't afraid to admit it. She was the past I'd left behind. She was Cuba. Mi Cuba querida, el son montuno . . .

Blackout.

Carmelita is sitting on a chair inside the cube wearing a hat made of helium balloons. A square spotlight resembling a film close-up is on her face. As the scene proceeds more light bathes the stage.

CARMELITA

The doctor said hypnosis might help. I said, "Anything doctor, anything for a cure." So he started to hypnotize me but in the middle of it he said I had to count backwards. Backwards. I got this sharp pain in my throat and I felt these blood clots in my mouth and I said, "No, Doctor, I can't count backwards. Don't make me. Count backwards. I never count backwards." The doctor writes in his chart: "Subject is mathematically impaired." They wanted to know what other impairments I got. So they connected these wires to my brain, my computer, my mango Macintosh. The doctors, they monitor my every move.

This (pointing to deflated balloons) is connected to my organizational skills, this to my musical memory, and this to my housecleaning ability. This (pointing to an extra large balloon) is linked to my libido. When I think of Soraya my nurse giving me a sponge bath or rubbing Keri lotion on my chest it (pops balloon with hidden pin so audience does not see) pops uncontrollably. And this one (pointing to a regular-sized balloon) is for languages. Spieglein Spieglein on der Wand. Wer is die schonste im ganzen land. . . . What language is dis? Is this the language of Jung und Freud? Oh herren and herrleins pierce me with your key. Let me not be a question mark any more. Open up Pandora's box.

The doctors they tell me my name is (pronouncing the name with an American accent) Carmelita Tropicana. I've had a terrible accident. I hurt my head when I was chocolate-pudding wrestling. I don't remember a thing. (She sings) Remember, walking in the sand, remember her smile was so inviting, remember . . . I don't remember the lyrics to this song. So much flotsam and jetsam inside my head. And I want to remember so much I get these false attacks. In desperation, I appropriate others' memories.

The doctors try to control these attacks by surrounding me with familiar things. (Shows bottle-cap necklace) This beautiful bottle cap says "Tropicana, shake well"—I don't know. Then they tell me to eat the food they bring, because the French philosopher Proust ate one madeleine cookie and all his childhood memories came rushing back to him. (Picking up a can of Goya beans) Goy . . . Goya? Black beans. (Picking up beverage bottle) Malta Hatuey or is it Hatuey? Is the H aspirated or not aspirated? And is he the chief Indian Hatuey or the Native American Hatuey? Oh, these labels are so confusing. (Picking up a yuca) Is this a yuca or a yuucka? Do I eat it or do I beat it? Oh to be or not to be. But who, that is the question.

That short guy with the cigar—what was his name, Pingalito, the one who made me throw up on the bed—he tells me I'm from Cuba.

Maybe there is only one way to find out. To go back to the place I was born in. My homeland, the place that suckled me as a newborn babe. In the distance, I hear the clink, clink, clink of a metal spoon against glass. It is my mami stirring condensed milk with water. She holds a glass. The milk beckons me. I hear a song: "How Would You Like to Spend the Weekend in Havana?" (Carmelita takes off balloon hat. Lights change. Carmelita speaks into the microphone.)

My journey begins at five A.M. at the Miami airport. I am so sleepy. It's crazy to be at the airport at five A.M. I don't know where I am going; I hear "Follow the Maalox, follow the Maalox" and then I spot a multitude. The Cuban diaspora that's going back, holding onto plastic bags with medicines and the most magnificent hats. I am so underdressed. These people are so dressed: skirts on top of pants on top of skirts. The gentleman in front of me, an octogenarian, has his head down. I don't know if it's age or the weight of his three hats. I discover my people are a smart people. They can weigh your luggage and limit you to forty-four pounds, but they cannot weigh your body. The layer look is on.

The excitement mounts when I enter the plane. The doctors told me to be careful. Too much, too soon can cause attacks. In only forty-five minutes I will cross an ocean of years.

When we land it is scorching hot outside. People desperately rip off the layers on the tarmac. I see a field in the distance. Palm trees, two peasants, and an ox. It reminds me of Southeast Asia, Vietnam. I never been there. But who knows where memories come from—movies, books, magazines.

I go to the counter in the airport holding on to my Cuban passport, my American passport, and a fax saying my visa is waiting for me here. Names are called for people with visas but mine is not one. The immigration guy says I gotta go back. Say what? You know who I am? He says "Who?" Yo soy Cecilia Valdés . . . Oh my god. I started to sing an operetta, a zarzuela. The guy thinks I am making fun of him. I say no. I'm sorry. I say I hurt my head and it has affected my vocal chords. He don't care. I am returned. Back to El Norte. But I don't care because I have determination. I go back especially now that I know how to dress. I go in style. I make myself a magnificent hat. Check it out. (Carmelita models hat.)

Soy una tienda ambulante. In my Easter bonnet with toilet paper on it. I'm a walking Cuban department store. Tampons and pearls, toilet paper, stationery supplies. What a delight. (The actress steps out of the white cube and, dropping Carmelita's Spanish accent, addresses the audience.) Now this is the part where you think it's performance art, a joke. Truth is stranger than fiction. *The New York Times* in 1993 had a photo essay of women with these hats. And when I went back the competition got tougher. Next to me was a woman with a pressure cooker on her head. A pressure cooker. These people are going to survive. (As she returns the microphone, she resumes the Carmelita persona.)

When I go back, the immigration guy is so friendly. "Back so soon? I like your hat." So I give him a couple of tampons.

I take a taxi to the Hotel Capri. I tell my driver Francisco I want to see, touch, feel, hear, taste Cuba. All my orifices are open. Francisco says: "No es fácil." It's not easy. I have come during the special period. The special period—that's what the government calls it. No gas, no electricity, no food. I look out the window. Cubans are all on bicycles. They look like skinny models. Francisco says when there is no gasoline and the buses are not running he fuels his body with water with sugar. Water with sugar. The great Cuban energizer. Agua con azúcar and then he can walk for miles.

When I arrive in the Hotel Capri I go to the dining room. I can tell who the Cubans are with relatives here. They are the ones wrapping up food. I meet María Elena who is here for a conference and is wrapping chicken, bread, cheese. I ask her what about eggs. Don't forget the eggs. She says, "Eggs. Qué va. Yesterday I had to give a lecture on the poet Julián del Casal and when I took the paper out of my briefcase there was egg yolk all over. Egg yolk all over. No es fácil. It is not easy."

The taped voice of writer is heard as the actress goes to the dimly lit space and puts on lipstick.

WRITER

Sometimes New York is too much. So is Havana. I toured the colonial part of the city. Kids flocked to me for candy, gum. Two decrepit mangy dogs limped along the cobblestones. Two guys tried to sell me a potent drug, PPG. Makes the man potent, satisfy your woman. A girl about fourteen asks me for my pintalabios. I part with my Revlon number forty-four "Love that Red" lipstick. I eat at La Bodeguita with two Cuban artists, a meal of fried yuca, fried pork, fried bananas. Cholesterol is not a problem. I take a ride to my hotel in a private vintage Chevrolet circa 1955, rumbling as it plods through streets, darkened except for a building blindingly bright, a beacon of light, the Spanish embassy. And the new currency is the dollar. Five dollars for the ride, five dollars for the beer at the hotel lobby. And who do I see coming in, Pintalabios, Revlon number forty-four, looking good with a man. What is she doing with that man and my lipstick? She looks down when she sees me. I'm pissed, but with a swig of beer, reconsider, maybe the lipstick got her a steak dinner. And I go to my room, place a call to New York and put the TV on. CNN news. And the call comes through, and I switch channels. A movie is beginning: *The Green Berets*. I am in Cuba watching *The Green Berets*.

Carmelita goes to the cemetery. A Cuban son is playing as Carmelita enters the white space.

CARMELITA

I have been in Havana for three days and I don't have any flashback, not even an attack. I decide to go visit my relatives, the dead ones at the cemetery. Maybe they'll talk to me from the grave. El cementerio de Colón is a beautiful cemetery with big trees that give shade and lots of statues and mausoleums. I start to look for the Tropicanas, but find Menocales, Menéndez instead. Menéndez brothers? I see four seniors hanging out by the tombstones. They look like they're in their seventies—two men and a couple. I go ask if they know the Tropicanas. They don't, but they are very curious about me and start to ask me my name, what I do, where I live. When I say New York, they all say "Nueva York!" The woman, Consuelo, looks at my nose.

CONSUELO

José, mira que se parece a Luisita. De la nariz pa' abajo. Exactica. You look like my niece Luisita. She's a very smart girl, a painter. She went to New York last year. Went to all the museums. She was fascinated, fascinated. All those restaurants you have! Japanese, Chinese, even Filipino! She said the food, that was the real art. She came back twenty pounds heavier and her work changed. She went from Abstract to Realism. I have a new painting hanging in my living room. It's a triptych of desserts. There's a strawberry cheesecake, crème brûlée, y cake de chocolate. Está lindo, lindo.

JOSÉ

(Gradually becoming more and more distressed) Carmencita, you don't know this but Consuelito here used to be obese. Obese. A diabetic with a sweet tooth. ¡Imagínate! Now in nine months of the special period she has lost ninety pounds. No es fácil. No es fácil.

CONSUELO

José, your blood pressure y el stress.

JOSÉ

Chica, déjame hablar. How am I going to get rid of el stress unless I talk? Mira, Carmencita, people here are doing everything to survive. They are keeping roosters, chickens. Animals right here in Havana. ¡Animales! Pa' que contar . . . (sound of crackling fire)

On tape there are the sounds of a stampede, horses neighing, flamenco music, and crickets. A red spotlight comes on.

ARRIERO

I was born in Badajoz, España. Todo era tranquilidad. Un sueño dulce. The sky clear, not a cloud in the sky for miles except for the clouds of dust me and Dulcinea made as we galloped across the dry fields. The sun was strong. One day it rained and the mud spattered from our pasterns to our forearms. When I turned two my master told me I had been sold to a conquistador. A conquistador, what a strange and exciting sound. The day came when I had to leave Spain and become a stallion. The stallion of a conquistador. But I was too excited that night to sleep. (whinnies). We horses are a bit high-strung. I stayed up with my mother counting stars. At daybreak she gave me her bendición. "Arriero, from now on you will be counting stars in the New World."

I was one of the first horses to set hoof in the New World. And I should have known from the voyage from Spain to Cuba what was to happen. All of us animals herded into a tiny ship. The roosters that climbed on my back, the rats I had to stomp on. But the worst was the boredom. Nowhere to go. Couldn't stretch my legs. Always fed the same thing, hay and oats, hay and oats, for variety I ate my own dung. I thought the voyage would never end. I started counting the days. Uno, dos, tres, cuatro. I gave up. I fell into such a depression and there was no Prozac in those days. Then somebody yelled: "Land. Land!" It was the island of Cuba. I couldn't believe my 340-degree degree peripheral vision. Grass everywhere. And trees with fruit: guanábanas, mangoes, mameys. And the natives were so friendly they walked around smoking offering us cigars: Partagás, Panetela. Camel Light. No thank you. I don't smoke. But I will have some of that yuca barbecue. Yuca barbecue was my favorite. I hated the guinea pig. I'm a vegetarian.

Havana in those days was teeming with life, especially the mosquito kind. I couldn't swat them fast enough with my tail, which is why I hated Gonzaga the priest that kept plucking the hairs out of my tail to make hair shirts, hair shirts to give to the natives as gifts. Gonzaga was not my master—it's just that I was given to him for a little while. I was on loan because of my name Arriero: the one who can carry much weight. And joder, that priest was fat. It took three men to put him on my back.

That day we were delivering the hair shirts is when we saw the chief Indian Hatuey. There was smoke in the distance. I didn't want to go because I know where there's smoke there's fire, but Gonzaga saw some of his fellow priests and we had to go. There was a crowd gathered, so much commotion we couldn't hear but I rotated my left ear and heard a priest say to Hatuey, "Repent, repent, and if you will—you will go to heaven. If not, hell." Hatuey looked at the priest and said, "If heaven is where the Spanish Christians go, I'll take hell." And the flames took Hatuey. Right there. I saw it. And so much more. I saw so many Indians die, so many. So many dead Indians from disease and overwork. I thought of my mother's farewell words, "Arriero, from now on you will be counting stars in the New World." No mother, not stars.

The red spotlight crossfades into flickering lights and then returns to bright.

CARMELITA

Ai, my head. I must have fallen into a CUMAA. A Collective Unconscious Memory Appropriation Attack. I need an aspirin. When I take out the Bayer aspirins, the four seniors yell "Bayer." Like they have never seen an aspirin. So we decide to divide the one hundred thirty-five aspirins into four seniors. Some fall on the ground. It is too much, so the men take the ones that fell on the floor and Consuelo takes the bottle. As I am leaving José Miguel says:

JOSÉ

Do you pray? Do you believe? I do. Every day. If I didn't I'd be dead.

Slow fade to black.

An audiotape is heard with the following joke.

Did you hear the one about the eggs and the fried steak? There are these eggs running through the Malecón Boulevard in Havana. And they're running because they are being chased by a million hungry Cubans. And these eggs are running and the Cubans are after them. And as the eggs are running they pass in front of a fried steak that is sitting on the wall of the Malecón, very relaxed. And the eggs yell at the steak, "The Cubans are coming, the Cubans are coming! Aren't you afraid they'll come get you?" The steak says, "No way, these Cubans don't know what a steak looks like."

The stage is dark as slides of Havana are projected onto a screen. The writer reads into the mike and when the slide of her old house comes on she stops reading and speaks into the mike, pointing out the different parts of the house.

WRITER

(Slide of Cuban countryside.) As I go sightseeing I try to strike up a conversation with everyone I meet. But when people ask me where I'm from I have a certain trepidation. How will I be received? I lie. I begin by telling them my father is Puerto Rican. After five minutes I feel comfortable enough to tell them I was born here, but don't remember much.

(Slide of Cuban plaza with flag.) I am like a tourist in my own country. Everything is new. I walk everywhere hoping I will recall something. Anything. I have this urge to recognize and be recognized. To fling my arms around one of those ceiba trees and say, I remember you from the park when I went with Cristobalina my nanny who had Chinese eyes, kinky hair, and used to sing, "Reloj, no marques las horas."

(Slide of cemetery.) I want a crack on the sidewalk to open up and say, yes, I saw you when you jumped over in your patent leather shoes holding on to your grandfather's index finger. But it doesn't happen. There is no recognition from either the tree or the sidewalk. . . .

(Slide of aerial view of Havana.) So I do what most Cubans do when they go back. I go back to the house I was born in. Trescientos diecinueve de la calle ocho entre quinta y tercera. The address pops out as if I'd been there yesterday.

(Slide of Centro Gallego.) I'm nervous. Why? It's just a house.

(Slide of house.) Oh my God. There it is. The house I was born in. (Pointing to various images on the screen) There was a patch of dirt here and in this corner there was a slug. I used to poke him with a stick. The slug, he's gone. And on this side I planted my mango tree. We had invented a new game, "agrarian reform" and had to cultivate the land. It was by the mango tree that I had an epiphany. I was poking at the ground to see how my mango tree was doing when I heard her footsteps. She had long hair tied into a pony tail, red lips, and dreamy eyes like a cow. I ran to her and jumped on her and kissed her creamy cheeks. "Okay, okay," she said, putting me down. We looked at each other for an instant. I ran and hid by my mango tree. My heart was beating fast, I was sweating. I knew then that that was no ordinary kiss. That kiss would mean a lot more in years to come.

And it was in this balcony that we played with our live Easter chicks. Live chicks dyed purple, pink, and green. We left my cousin Teresa with the chicks while we went to make skirts for them from plastic ruffled cookie wrappers, and when we came back Teresa was throwing the last chick from the balcony to its death. And on this porch we used to play Tarzan and Jane. I begged for a human part but I was told I had to play the cheetah or the elephant. I was playing cheetah when my father came. I called him the stranger because he had been away fighting in the revolution. He gave me and my sister gold bullet shells.

(Slide of stairs.) I couldn't wait to go inside. Those are the stairs, the stairs I fell from when I was six months old. I bolted upstairs to my bedroom.

(Slide of writer by door.) Two men are in the middle of a business meeting. I interrupt. I'm sorry. I used to sleep here. The woman who has been following me, the secretary, tells me I can't just barge in as if it's my house. You don't understand, I say, this was my house. She opens the door to the bathroom.

(Slide of bathroom.) Oh my bidet, my toilet. She says, "Hey, you're not one of those Cubans who plans to come back and take over their house." I say, "Oh no, we only rented." The moment I say this I feel like I'm not like one of those Cubans who left—who never would have said they rented. They wouldn't have said they owned just one house. Are you kidding me, we owned the whole block.

(Slide of construction.) My house is now a construction company. Privatization entering Cuba right through this, my house.

Carmelita enters the white cube as a romantic ballad plays.

CARMELITA

It's the middle of the afternoon. There's music playing. From the window I see the Hotel Nacional as it sits on a rock and overlooks all of Havana Bay. I think of having a mojito, the favorite drink of Papa Hemingway. It could also be mine since I don't remember what it tastes like. I walk to the renovated, four-star Hotel Nacional smelling the delicious grass. The sun is trying to come out. It just rained. I walk to the entrance of the hotel. The doorman winks. I say, "Buenas tardes." Inside it is cool and beautiful. There are potted palm trees, Spanish leather chairs, and blue tile. Blue tile. How I hate blue tile, especially with yellow squiggles. It doesn't go with anything. Bad decorating choice. A hotel employee looks at me. The blue tiles are making me sick. I'm holding tight to the potted palm frond.

DOCTOR

Carmelita, suéltala. Let go. Let go of your mother's hand. You have to be brave. Hay que tener coraje, mucho coraje en la vida.

CARMELITA

No. Mami. No Mami. Please don't let go of me. I'm your child. I want to be with you Mami. I don't want to go with the green man.

MOTHER

Carmelita, it's just a green uniform. Mi hijita. Don't be afraid. It will be over soon.

HOTEL EMPLOYEE

Señorita, if you don't let go of the palm frond, I'm going to have to call security.

CARMELITA

I'm sorry. Yes. I don't feel well. I need to eat. I'm hungry. I have to sit down in the dining room and eat. I go into the dining room like a somnambulist following the song "Lágrimas Negras" played by a trio. Where have I heard "Lágrimas Negras" played by a trio like this?—Oh yes, last week in Gloria Estefan's Miami restaurant. At least the short-term memory works. I should try to remember. The more I remember the more I will remember. Let's see, what did I learn today? Ochún is the goddess of the sea. No, that's Yemayá. And if you want to get the love of your life you have to leave honey on a plate under your bed for five days. You get the love you want and the cucarachas you don't. And the slang word for dyke is bombera, firefighter. So maybe if I yell, "Fire, fuego," would all the dykes come out now? I feel much better. So much better I order a mojito and pork sandwich. "La Última Noche que Pasé Contigo" is playing. The waiter brings me the sandwich. He has a green jacket on. I try not to look at his green uniform. Trembling, I pick up the sandwich. A slice falls, no, it jumps.

Pig flies in and hangs above Carmelita's head. On tape is the sound of a squealing pig.

PIG

(Snort, snort) The horse thought it was bad in colonial times, he should talk. I was a pig in the special period. Cochinito Mamón. I was just two weeks old lying under my mother's belly sucking her sweet milk with my brothers and sisters when I was yanked off her tit by a man who put a blanket over my head and took me from my farm in Santiago to live in an apartment in Havana. It was so quick I couldn't even say good-bye to my family. The apartment was on the second floor. My legs were too short. I couldn't go up the stairs. Señor, I am no goat. I went into the apartment. I looked for mud but everything was so clean. The woman in the apartment, the wife, cradled me in her arms calling me "Nene," boy. She fed me milk in the bottle. Hey lady, I'm not into rubber. I want real nipples. The man complained about my smell, so everyday she had to give me a bath in the tub.

WOMAN

Nene, sit still, Nene, don't splash, Nene, let me wipe your nose.

PIG

I'm not a boy, I'm a pig, (squealing) I'm a pig! One day the man came in walking funny. He had been drinking with his brother who worked at the Hotel Nacional. He smacked the wife on the rump and made her get the tape measure from her sewing kit. He put it around my belly.

MAN

¡Coño, qué gordo está este puerco! This pig is fat.

PIG

I could smell the rum on his breath. She should give him a bath. The phone rang. It was long distance, the relatives from the United States. The man said something about showing me to them. The next day was Sunday. I didn't know what was happening. The woman put a hat on my head. It was a gift from a cousin in New York. A baseball cap. It kept falling off, so she tied it with another gift she got from New York: a bungee chord. The chord was tight around my neck. She was sitting on a chair holding me on her lap, lifting my head to look up. The man quickly got behind us when a flash went off. I got scared. I didn't know it was supposed to be a family portrait. I jumped down. My hoof ripped her panty hose. I tried to run but I had put on some weight. I slid behind a table and knocked over a lamp. It broke. The man went after me. He was screaming:

MAN

¡Puerco, puerco de mierda!

PIG

She was screaming:

WOMAN

¡Nene! ¡Nene!

PIG

I was squealing: ¡Mami! ¡Mami! With all the noise, the neighbors, they knocked on the door.

NEIGHBORS

¿Qué pasa? ¿Qué pasa?

PIG

The man flew across the room and tackled me. He whispered in my ear.

MAN

Coño, puerco de mierda. You are going to be roast pork, but before that we are going to cut your vocal chords so you don't squeal and disturb the neighbors anymore.

PIG

The next day I was put in a box. The woman was crying as she punched holes in the box so I could see. We got to the place. I could see blue tiles.

DOCTOR

Carmelita, relájate. Estamos en la sala. I'm going to put this on so you can breathe deep. Respira profundo.

CARMELITA

No. I don't want to breathe.

DOCTOR

Déjate de tonterías, niña. Carmelita, quiero que cuentes. I want you to count backwards. Count backwards: 100, 99, 98 . . .

PIG

When I got out of the box, I saw a man in green. He had a shiny knife. I squealed, Mami! Mami! (Silent)

She pulls a string from the pig's neck and a stream of red glitter gushes down, spilling onto the white linoleum.

CARMELITA

My vocal chords, my tonsils. The pig and I, we had our operations at the same clinic. The clinic with blue tiles. I remember. We are all connected, not through AT&T, e-mail, Internet, but through memory, history, herstory, horsetory. I remember. (She shadowboxes as she recites the poem.)

I remember
Que soy de allá
Que soy de aquí
Un pie en New York (a foot in New York)
Un pie en La Habana (a foot in Havana)
And when I put a foot in Berlin (cuando pongo pata en Berlin)
I am called
A lesbische cubanerin
A woman of color
Culturally fragmented

Sexually intersected
But I don't split
I am fluid and interconnected
Like tie-dye colors I bleed
A Cuban blue sky into an American pumpkin orange
Que soy de allá
Que soy de aquí

Lights up bright

Hello people, you know me. I know you. I don't need no American Express card. I am Carmelita Tropicana, famous nightclub entertainer, superintendent, performance artist. And I am so happy to be here with you today, because ever since I was a little girl I ask my mami, When can I do a show called *Milk of Amnesia* at P.S. 122? And here I am. I am so lucky. Lucky I can dance un danzón, cantar un son, tener tremendo vacilón. Thanks to El Cochinito mamón, sandwich de lechón. I got to exit with a song, sabrosón like the sandwich de lechón. (She exits singing and dancing.)

Cochinito mamón
Sandwich de lechón
Cochinito mamón
Sandwich de lechón

Lights fade down. Audiotape with writer's voice comes on.

WRITER

September 1993. I met an American lawyer who is here in Cuba to witness a period of "transition." It seems in 1993 anything can happen. In the theatre festival there were plays that were critical of the system and played to packed houses. I thought by coming to Cuba I would have answers. Instead I have more questions.

These are *Star Trek* glasses. They form rainbows around everything you look at. Am I looking at Cuba from an American perspective? No es fácil. It's not easy to have clear vision. In seven days I can only get sound bites. Cuba is a land of contradictions.

No one is homeless in Cuba, although homes are falling apart. Everyone gets health care, but there is no medicine. There is only one newspaper, but everyone is educated. No conspicuous consumerism. The dollar is legal, but there's the U.S. embargo. The clothes are threadbare, vivid colors now turned pastel. So much food for the soul, none for the belly.

I don't want to keep score. It's not a competition. Cuba vs. the U.S. When the Olympics are on I'm at a loss as to who to root for. . . . No, not really. I root for Cuba. Why? Is it that I'm for the underdog and that if I'm in the U.S. I am more Cuban and if I'm in Cuba I'm more American? Is Cuba my wife and America my lover or the other way around? Or is Cuba my biological mami and the U.S. my adopted mom?

As lights go bright, Carmelita enters the white cube.

CARMELITA

My journey is complete. My amnesia is gone. After so many years in America, I can drink two kinds of milk. The sweet condensed milk of Cuba and the Grade A, pasteurized, homo kind from America.

My last day in Cuba I spend at an artist's house. We sit, ten of us, in a circle, all sipping our one bottle of rum. I turn to the man next to me and tell him I have one regret. I didn't hear any Cuban music and to me Cuba is music. He smiles. He is Pedro Luis Ferrer, famous composer, musician. He will play me his songs, but first he tells me, "The embargo is killing us."

(Stepping out of Carmelita character and addressing the audience) I agree with Pedro Luis and I want to leave you with a song by him called "Todos por lo Mismo," a song that says it best:

Everybody for the same thing
Between the pages of colonialism
Capitalists, homosexuals, atheists, spiritualists, moralists
Everybody for the same thing

The tape plays several choruses as Carmelita exits.

Chicas 2000

Chicas 2000 was first performed at Dixon Place with commissioning funds from the Joyce Mertz Gilmore Foundation in 1997 and was later presented at Performance Space 122 in 1998. It was directed by Uzi Parnes, designed by Charles Scott Richard, and stage managed by Nicole Mitchell.

Cast

Pingalito Betancourt/Carmelita Tropicana: herself
Desiree Delgado/Clana: Ana Margaret Sánchez
Dr. Igor: Uzi Parnes
Rodesia/Cluna: Rebecca Sumner Burgos
Additional voices on tape: Guinevere Turner, Rachel Miskowiec, Charles Scott Richard

Setting

Chicas 2000 takes place in 1999, 2013, and 2014.

The action takes place in

A TV studio where Carmelita's show is being taped
Dr. Igor's laboratory
The Behaviour Modification Unit
The Free Zone
The Streets of Chusmatown
The Chusmatic Wrestling Casino

Glossary

Chusma: loud, gross, tacky and excessive behavior, tasteless with attitude, similar to white trash, only people-of-color trash
Chusmatown: Ghetto where Chusmas live in 2013
BMU: Behaviour Modification Unit, a prison of the future
Humani: human/animal transplant, a new species
Coño: Spanish curse word referring to women's privates, a word as overused as the English *F* word

Scene 1

The action of the play begins in the present time at a cable TV studio, where Carmelita Tropicana, a nightclub entertainer, is taping her variety show. Sitting in the studio audience is Dr. Igor, who fidgets throughout. A video camera and a monitor are on one side. There is a curtain with "CHICAS 2000" colorfully written on it. An announcer's voice is heard offstage.

ANNOUNCER

Ladies and gentlemen, welcome to Carmelita Tropicana's *CHICAS 2000*. To start the show, we have the winner of our Hoi Polloi contest: retired transportation official, Pingalito Betancourt.

A man dressed in a typical Cuban guayabera shirt, chomping on a cigar, enters the stage and stands in front of the curtain.

PINGALITO

Good evening. It is an honor to be here in the segment called Opinions of the Hoi Polloi. When Carmelita ax me to do Hoi Polloi, I got excited. I thought it is Spanish Hoy Pollo—Today Chicken—but no, Hoi Polloi is an expression that means mi gente, the people, the masses.

I want to discuss with you my philosophy about Puritanism.

I started investigating Puritanism last Thanksgiving when I was eating turkey and watching *Pocahontas*. I know you look at me and see a very Puritan kind of guy, a regular John Smith. Well that is correct. I have many of the components of Puritanism: self-reliance, industry, and frugality.

Let's take self-reliance first. You see these glasses of mine are broken. I relied on myself to fix them with a little duck tape and safety pin.

Industry. Yes, America should have many many factories.

Three. Frugality. El dos por uno, two for the price of one. When I can go to the A&P supermarket and buy two containers of Tropicana orange juice for the price of one, it floats my boat, and rocks my boots.

But where I part company with Puritanism is with the sexuality stuff. I think there is a little hypocrisy here. How many of you remember Dr. Joycelyn Elders, eh?

Please raise your hands.

For those of you who did not raise your hands, I will tell you.

Dr. Joycelyn Elders was the Surgeon General who dared to mention masturbation. And what happened when she mention masturbation? She got fired. Now, I want to take a poll today. Raise your hands, ladies and gentlemen, if you have never touched yourself. Come on, go ahead. Maybe the camera can take a close-up of the audience. Okay.

So people, Puritanism has some good things and some bad. How do we save it? How do we create a gentler, kinder Puritanism? We cannot throw out the baby with the bathwater. No.

I was thinking of this when the answer came to me watching a PBS special on the bonobo monkeys of the Congo. The bonobo monkeys are incredible. Distant cousins, you say. Not so distant. We share ninety-eight percent of the same genes. Like us they got tools.

You should see these monkeys with a Black and Decker power saw.

And they have culture. One bonobo monkey, Jane, was taught to paint. She already has two shows at a Soho Art Gallery. The critics call her paintings Japanese Simian.

But the bonobos excel us in two areas. First government. The ERA, they got it. A girl or boy bonobo can become king or queen. And sex, hah. They have sex for recreation, procreation, to relieve stress, anxiety, and boredom.

Can you imagine, ladies and gentlemen, what a world this would be if you got up in the morning and your doorbell rang. It's the UPS girl. You are tired and sleepy and to wake you up she starts to rub up against you. And then you go to the Post Office and you lick your stamps and the Postal Employee starts to lick you. And then you go to the bank. You are overdrawn in your checking account and you are so upset that the bank teller, to make you feel better, starts to fondle your privates.

What a world this could be ladies and gentlemen. I say, Let us invigorate America by creating a real banana bonobo republic (scratches his crotch).

Now let us bring out Desiree Delgado for a commercial message on a very important subject for us men.

As Pingalito exits, music comes on and Desiree, dressed as the Piagra Goddess, enters slowly, dancing to the music.

DESIREE

Impotent men
I am the goddess
I bring you the pie

That packs the power.
(She shows the audience the pie.)
Piagra
If your dysfunction is erectile
Piagra gives you a harder-than-steel projectile
Remember the pie that packs the power: Piagra

As she exits, Dr. Igor, dressed in an overcoat, tries to get Desiree's attention.

DR. IGOR

Mademoiselle, I have plastic roses for Carmelita. She loves plastic.

DESIREE

You again, sit down. Sit, we're doing a show.

Intro music comes on as Carmelita enters dancing.

CARMELITA

Hello people. Feeling good? I am, because you know what happens in the year 2000? Latinos will be the majority in the U.S.A. The majority minority. So many Latinos, so much love. And we can see why. Latinos are penetrating the culture through all the orifices. There is penetration through the ear with the music, through the mouth with the food, through the tongue with the tongue. Una penetración total. Oh, I can feel the amor across the land from the redwood forest to the Caribbean waters. Together in this new millennium, let's make the magic real.

Let's begin to make the magic real with the segment of the show called "Homo Decorum." We will be creating a gift perfect for any occasion: a kindergarten graduation, a rocky divorce, or a triple bypass surgery. This gift will tell them how much you care.

Let me bring out my assistant Desiree. (Desiree sexily struts out with a paper bag.)

Desiree will help to show how easy it is to make. The tools of the trade, your lips and mouth. In this case Desiree's.

Camera come for a close-up of Desiree's lips and mouth which she will be using. (Carmelita points to Desiree's mouth.)

And now the raw material. (Desiree takes out the mango from the bag.)

The mango. El mango. Let's begin. (Desiree is about to bite the mango and Carmelita stops her.)

Ah, ah. What did I tell you? Mango stains never come off so what you gotta do?

DESIREE

Take off my shirt.

CARMELITA

Take off her shirt. What a smart girl! Now, ladies and gentlemen, this is another surprise for you. Check out the brassiere Desiree is wearing. It is another by-product of this creation. As you can see, the brassiere is stained like the modern paintings of Jackson Pollock, who they used to call Jack the Dripper, before he sold his paintings for millions. Camera can come for a close-up of the bra. (Carmelita points to both breasts.)

It is beautifully stained in mango and chocolate. Go ahead, Desiree, begin. (Desiree begins to bite the mango, spitting the peel on the floor, and sucks it, making loud slurping sounds as juice falls down her chin.)

While she works let me show you what other supplies you will need. (Carmelita takes out magic markers from the brown paper bag which she shows to the audience.)

Magic markers in red, black, orange, green. Now let's look at another pit Desiree worked on this morning. Look how clean. She is good, don't you think?

We use the magic markers to decorate this pit, and let me show you what the gift will look like. (Carmelita takes out the Mango Pet from her bra.)

Voilà, the ecologically correct, user-friendly, perfect for any occasion, utilitarian—I ate it before I make it the Mango Pet. What a masterpiece. Please, the camera can come for a close-up of this beautiful creation. Camera, where are you going, camera . . . Ven acá. . . . ¿Qué pasa?

Lights dim. A voice is heard offstage.

POLICE

Ms. Tropicana? FBI's DNA RA. This studio is shut down for violating Live Active Culture Penal Code XX69.

CARMELITA

What?

POLICE

You have the right to remain silent. You have the right to an attorney.

Carmelita exits and Dr. Igor, in the audience, rushes with her backstage.

DR. IGOR

Wait, I can help, I'm a doctor.

New Age music plays and fades as new scene begins.

Scene 2

In the dark, a voice is heard offstage. It is a newscast of the following infomercial.

NEWSCAST WOMAN

On December 31, 1999, TV shows like these were taken off the air. They were symbolic of the social ills gripping the nation. It was in response to these shows that the FBI DNA RA BMU was created: The DNA Remodeling Agency and Behavior Modification Units. Its mission: to better the human race through designer genes. Genes responsible for antisocial behavior were coded and classified. Among the deviant genes heading the list: the chusma gene which gives rise to a disease known as chusmería—shameless, loud, gross, tacky behavior, in short, tasteless with attitude. (Two chusma women come out and a spotlight comes on.)

Individuals with the chusma gene are known to favor Egyptian head movement from side to side. (One of the women illustrates this movement.)

They wear clothes that are too tight for their weight category with emphasis on their chest and posterior. (One of the women shows her ass and touches her breast.)

And when excited they are known for wild gesticulations of their extremities. (They both illustrate, gesticulating wildly.)

The chusma gene is found in Latin America, with high concentration in the Caribbean, although the chusma gene has crossed over to North America. U.S. citizens classified with the gene are: Dennis

Rodman, Roseanne, Tanya Harding, and Martha Stewart. The latter is a perfect example of the gene in remission. Although the chusma gene cannot be eradicated or its disease cured, it can be controlled. The government has stepped up its efforts to combat the chusma gene and a disease called (both women yell) chusmería.

The women go into the audience and ad lib.

CHUSMA WOMAN

We should make a citizen's arrest, your clothes are really offensive. Mira, esta gente no se sabe vestir pa' na'.

Scene 3

Dr. Igor's apartment and laboratory. A curtain is painted with large test tubes and laboratory instruments. Carmelita, in a white dress resembling a nightgown, is tied to a column. Dr. Igor, wearing a lab coat, is with her. Hollywood B-movie score plays as scene begins.

CARMELITA

No . . . no. . . .

DR. IGOR

But I bailed you out.

CARMELITA

Let go of me, coño. (She struggles to get free.)

DR. IGOR

Coño, what a sweet word, music to my ears. A real chusma.

CARMELITA

Don't.

DR. IGOR

Why not, that's what you are. That's why they took you off the air. It's what I like. You see, I was born into a world of elite effete. Cold, dull, gray, French tailored gabardine suits. Something was missing. I had this je ne sais quoi feeling. And then I saw your show. It was a world full of color, plastic, grease. I want you. (He kneels down beside her and grabs her.)

CARMELITA

How many times do I have to say no? Can't you take a hint?

DR. IGOR

Oh poppycock!

CARMELITA

I say no cock, papi.

DR. IGOR

Chérie, you are not giving me a chance. Let me give you my profile. I am French, Caucasian, Virgo. I like to take long walks around the aisles of the supermarkets. My hobbies are creative experimentation and watching your show over and over and over. I have them all on tape. Now will you have me?

CARMELITA

If I could love a man, it would be you. But I am not that way.

DR. IGOR

If you won't have me, I will have you one way or another.

CARMELITA

What do you mean?

DR. IGOR

I'll give you un clue. Hello Dolly.

CARMELITA

Hello Dolly, it's so nice to have . . .

DR. IGOR

No. Dolly . . .

CARMELITA

Parton.

DR. IGOR

No. Dolly . . .

CARMELITA

Lama.

DR. IGOR

Oh mon Dieu. Let me show you. I took part in the genome project of Dr. Watson, decoding DNA. I was the one to identify the chusma gene. And then they classified it as a deviant gene. I had to leave the project and set up my own laboratory. I have been conducting experiments. (He opens his coat to show purple marshmallow Peeps.) Observe. All have the same color, markings, eyes. All identical bunny rabbits.

CARMELITA

¡Qué cute!

DR. IGOR

I cloned them. You leave me no choice.

CARMELITA

Oh, my God, you can't. That's a nonconsexual act, it's taboo.

DR. IGOR

Taboo. You used to sing that. Soon I'll be hearing it from someone just like you.

CARMELITA

But cloning is illegal unless you're a billionaire or have a special dispensation from the Pope and Calvin Klein. You can't.

DR. IGOR

I will. Give me those buttocks. (He takes out a knife as she screams.)

CARMELITA

No, no . . . ah . . . (She faints.)

DR. IGOR

Oops. I cut too much. I'll make two. I'm man enough for two.

The same scary music that began the scene comes on, mixed with baby cries.

Nine months later at Dr. Igor's apartment laboratory. Dr. Igor is singing a lullaby to the tune of "Frère Jacques" as he holds a bassinet and rocks it back and forth.

DR. IGOR

Cluna, Clana, Cluna, Clana Chusma clones. Michael Jackson eat your heart out. I'm twice the daddy like you. (Carmelita enters holding a gun. Dr. Igor does not notice.) I made two clones from one.

CARMELITA

And that one has arrived. Give them to me.

DR. IGOR

No. I made them.

CARMELITA

From my butt cells.

DR. IGOR

I created them. They're mine.

CARMELITA

Babies are not possessions, like objects; they're alive. Give them to me. They belong to me.

DR. IGOR

You'll have to kill them and me.

Carmelita gets closer to him and he crosses her with the bassinet.

CARMELITA

Canalla. Eres un canalla.

DR. IGOR

I told you, I'd have you. This never would have happened if you had consented, if you'd given yourself to me.

CARMELITA

You cannot always take by brute force. Give them to me.

DR. IGOR

No.

CARMELITA

Have you no shame?

DR. IGOR

Shame! I'm proud. Look at them. (He holds two Barbie dolls with blue hair for her to see.)

CARMELITA

Oh, my God. What have you done? They're babies, not Barbies. They look like JonBenet Ramsey with all that makeup.

DR. IGOR

I've speeded up development. A little bit of hormones and makeup can't hurt.

CARMELITA

You disgust me. But I've been practicing with this laser stun gun at the shooting solarium. I'm a near-perfect shooter. What will it be? The kneecap. (He places the babies on his kneecap.) The groin. (He places the babies on his groin.) Or between the eyes. (He places the babies on his eyes as one baby pees on him.)

DR. IGOR

Oh, her peepee is blinding me.

Confused, Carmelita accidentally shoots him. At the same time, he throws the babies up in the air. He falls on the ground, hurt, and she catches the babies.

CARMELITA

Oh, my God. (Looking at Igor.)
What have I done?

BABIES

(Crying) Coño, coño.

CARMELITA

You sound just like me. And you look . . . This is too much. I feel at once nurturing and narcissistic. An identity crisis ripples over me.

Once a me, now a we. And what kind of relationship can I have? Am I your sister or your mother? Sister, mother, sister, mother. And what about the unthinkable, marriage between clones and bio-originals: abnormal and repugnant, or the way of the future? I must start a support group, but first let me change your diapers.

Police sirens and a policeman's voice are heard offstage.

POLICE

This is the police and the FBI's DNA RA BMU. Put down your weapons and come out. We got you surrounded. We know you have illegal clones in there. Come out.

CARMELITA

Forgive me, my clonies. There's already been too much bloodshed. Don't shoot, I'm coming out and I have innocent baby clones with me. Don't shoot (sobbing).

Scene 5

Gavel sounds begin the scene. Desiree, Carmelita's assistant, stands to face sentencing. There is a spotlight on her face. A judge's voice is heard offstage.

JUDGE

Desiree Delgado, I.D. 4321. Step forward. (She steps to the side.)

Forward. You have been found guilty of chusmería on two counts. One for your collaboration in the grotesque Homo Decorum. (Desiree cries.) Two. For aiding and abetting in the Mango Pet incident. You will serve an eight-year sentence in the Behavior Modification Unit in New Jersey off Route 17. Go to the end of the hall, Room D. Leave all your personal belongings. (She touches her earrings lovingly.) Including earrings, and pick up your uniform. And careful with the walk. We will be watching.

She walks half-chusma, sticking her butt out and swaying her hips, and half-repressed, sticking her butt in. Gavel sounds are heard. Lights out on Desiree as she exits.

Scene 6

Lights up on the other side of the stage as Carmelita enters the Behavior Modification Unit's testing area. She wears underwear, and carries her BMU uniform, which she will put on as the test is given. The voice of the female Testing Officer is heard offstage.

TESTING OFFICER

Proceed to the end of the hall for test number seventy-three. Answer the following questions. When a landlord places a building notice for all tenants, his note should read: To whom it may concern or to who it may concern? Who or whom? Whom or who?

CARMELITA

Who, whom, who cares?

TESTING OFFICER

State the medical reasons why a woman should shave, laser, or wax her armpits and bikini area?

CARMELITA

No reason. We like it bushy.

TESTING OFFICER

What detergent do you use on wooden floors: Mistolin, Mister Clean, or Murphy's Oil?

CARMELITA

Mistolin, Mistolin, mi abuelita . . .

TESTING OFFICER

Name the Hispanic group not known to throw garbage out the window.

CARMELITA

Hey, what you mean?

TESTING OFFICER

Repeat: Ask not what your country can do for you, Ask what you can do. Repeat ask, ask, ask.

The Testing Officer's questions begin to pick up speed.

CARMELITA

Ax, Ax. Lady, I said ax already.

TESTING OFFICER

Why did the Supreme Court rule that visual artists should never dip a crucifix in urine?

CARMELITA

It oxidizes the crufix.

TESTING OFFICER

Out of the following which is the preferred family pet: dalmatian, Labrador, standard poodle, Great Dane.

CARMELITA

Chihuahua with boxer mix.

TESTING OFFICER

Which would you rather attend: a chamber music concert at the Weinegerode Castle or a sweet sixteen birthday party with Tito Puente and Celia Cruz?

CARMELITA

It's sweet fifteen, of course, with Tito and Celia.

TESTING OFFICER

Now move into the Cochlea and Ear Measuring Center for gender preference calibration.

Atonal music comes on as Desiree joins Carmelita. They are both doing expressionistic moves, holding on to their ears. After a few minutes they bump into each other in the dark and recognize each other.

CARMELITA

Desiree, is it you? Is it you? (They sob and hug one another, overcome with emotion.)

DESIREE

Sí, it's me. I didn't think I would ever see you. It's been so long. Óyeme, chica, you made the headlines. The *Post* said: Star Clones Are Born. *El Diario:* Encuentran Chusma Clones. It was something, cause that day Fidel ate a Dole pineapple. His beard fell off. He looks twenty years younger, imagínate.

CARMELITA

Desiree, tell me about my clones. What happened to them?

DESIREE

All I know is what I read. They are not government-approved clones so they got sent to infant BMUs. One went to Miami, the other to . . . to . . .

CARMELITA

(Carmelita is so frustrated she shakes Desiree violently.) Think, think, think.

DESIREE

I'm trying. I can't think anymore. I don't know anything anymore.

CARMELITA

I know. We've been coded, decoded, encoded. Get a grip, girl. Here, take it and inhale. (She mimes a cigarette.)

DESIREE

A virtual cigarette. I never had one.

CARMELITA

You'll get used to it. Remember what I used to say: Make the magic real.

DESIREE

There's no magic here.

CARMELITA

No, but there is beauty. You're a fox in that outfit.

DESIREE

You think so? Oh, so are you.

CARMELITA

Let's look at the results from our testes. (She reads.) I.D. 008½. That's me. Inmate shows no artistic sensibility, but does show a propensity for manual labor, housecleaning and repressed heterosexuality (shocked).

DESIREE

A het! (Haughty) Excuse me. (She pushes Carmelita out of the way and reads her own results.) Inmate shows artistic genius, (proudly) a predisposition to law and macroeconomics, and latent bisexuality. Bisexual! (Upset.)

CARMELITA

And so it begins. The head games. The lies, their programming tactics. It's a stinking hand we got dealt.

DESIREE

Me lo dices.

Scene 7

Sounds of boot-camp marching songs. At another BMU space. A table and two chairs. On the table are martini glasses. Carmelita enters, reading a card, and goes to sit down in a chair.

CARMELITA

The esthetics of etiquette. Table Manners 101 again! When will I pass this? (She puts her elbow on the table and gets an electric shock.) Coño. (She gets another electric shock and cradles her hurt elbow. While she does so a woman, walking in a very manly way, comes in.)

RODESIA

Is this Table Manners 101?

CARMELITA

Yeah.

Rodesia turns the chair around so she can straddle it and gets several jolts.

CARMELITA

Be careful, the chair's electric. (Rodesia looks at the martini glass with the olives and dips her hand to take out the olive, stuffs it in her mouth and gets many electric jolts and spits out the olives at Carmelita.) Oh my, are you all right?

RODESIA

(Dazed) I don't know.

CARMELITA

I'll show you. I know this one. It's simulated martini. Hold the glass and make sure the pinky is sticking out. Sip, don't slurp. The toothpick picks up the trick olive with the pit. Now watch how I remove the pit without you seeing it. (She demonstrates as Rodesia watches, enthralled.)

RODESIA

You're good.

CARMELITA

Sometimes. The lobster dinner kills me. The bibs, butter, and those cracking instruments. They had to stop the class and give me mouth-to-mouth from all those electric shocks.

RODESIA

I don't understand all these rules. There's no fun in eating like this. My idea of a meal is going out to a stream and scooping up a salmon with your bare hands and biting the head off with eyes and everything.

CARMELITA

(Flirting) You like real sushi?

RODESIA

Yeah. I like fish. But there's only one problem: It always makes me crave those orgasmic pills.

CARMELITA

That's no problem. I've got some extras. Maybe we can take them together after Grammar and Syntax Correction class.

RODESIA

I don't have that class. Mostly I have Table Manners. Olfactory and Appetite Suppression classes.

CARMELITA

Old factory?

RODESIA

Desensitizing the sense of smell.

CARMELITA

Well, why don't you meet me at five o'clock under the simulated Japanese pond with the hologram of the 1984 thousand cloned frogs?

RODESIA

Uh, okay (unsure).

Scene 8

The BMU in Carmelita's cell. Carmelita and Rodesia are in the dark and we hear their sexual moans and groans. As Carmelita comes she gives out a high-pitched squeal. As the lights come up, they notice that the door of the cell has opened.

CARMELITA

(Apprehensively) Darling, go check the door.

RODESIA

(Rodesia goes to check the door.) There's no one.

CARMELITA

I'm glad I convinced you to sneak into my room. The way you bear-hugged that guard. That was something.

RODESIA

You weren't so bad yourself. The way you hit him with the shoe.

CARMELITA

Those pills do make you growl. Maybe next time we do it the natural way. I find myself very attracted to you, Rodesia. You have such animal magnetism. (Carmelita lightly grazes Rodesia's face. Rodesia recoils and gets up, moving away from her.)

RODESIA

Don't.

CARMELITA

Why not? I speak what's in my heart.

RODESIA

(Rodesia clutches her heart.) Heart. Oh, my God. I can't, I've tried.

CARMELITA

What is it, Rodesia?

RODESIA

I've tried to have relationships but they never work.

CARMELITA

Try me. I'm very understanding.

RODESIA

It can't happen. Don't you see? It would never work between us. You would never touch me, if you knew what I am (ashamed). You're a chusma (proudly) and I'm . . . I'm . . .

CARMELITA

Say it.

RODESIA

Woman-oso. I'm a transplant. Outside I'm all woman. Look at these breasts, this ass. But inside I have the heart of a little black bear.

CARMELITA

(To audience) I thought she was butch.

RODESIA

I'm a classified humani. Human-animal hybrid, woman-oso—woman-bear. In the winter I don't go out much, I sleep all the time.

CARMELITA

Well, that's three months. Like Sleeping Beauty.

RODESIA

There's more. I have a wild heart. Sometimes I have to stop myself from these impulses I have. I find myself alone in a subway station, someone asks me directions, the time. I get close to them. I start to smell. It's their scent that drives me crazy. I look at their fingers I can almost taste them. They don't even need hot sauce. I have to tear myself away. It's a struggle. (She assumes the pose of a bear and a woman repeatedly.) I'm both woman and bear, woman, bear, woman bear. (Growls) Human and animal (dejected).

CARMELITA

Humans are animals. You're a real animal that's all. You have to love yourself. You lack self-confidence, chica.

RODESIA

Love? I feel like a cannibal about to turn on my own people.

CARMELITA

There could be worse things, Rodesia. We can beat this thing together. Love and therapy conquer all.

RODESIA

You really do believe that. When I look into your eyes, I see a flicker of . . . of . . .

CARMELITA

(Carmelita bats her eyelashes while they hold hands.) Say it. I'll say it for you: hope. That's the one thing they cannot take away from us. Now it's my turn to confess. I got ten years for my chusmería, and five for shooting a man. I shot Dr. Igor for making illegal clones out of me. The police took my babies away. But I know one day we will be reunited and it will feel so good. I put up with a lot in this facility with the dream of that tomorrow. They are trying to make a bland woman out of me; well, I'll fake it. Like one fakes an orgasm.

RODESIA

You mean . . .

CARMELITA

No, darling, never with you. Trust me and believe in us. (Rodesia bares her teeth as she looks at Carmelita's hands, which she holds, and Carmelita stops her cannibalistic impulse.) There, there, my little teddy bear.

Rodesia kisses her hand. Sweet tinkling bells are heard.

Scene 9

A BMU space. Rodesia is falling asleep on a chair and Carmelita is trying to wake her up by shaking her. There is a table next to them.

CARMELITA

Ro, stay with me, work with me, baby.

Desiree enters crying, very upset, and goes to sit on the table next to Rodesia.

DESIREE

Ai, ai, ai.

CARMELITA

Not again, Desiree.

DESIREE

I can't take it.

CARMELITA

How long was it this time?

DESIREE

Three days.

CARMELITA

Three days! What were you wearing?

DESIREE

Chancletas. (She looks down and points at her tacky shoes with no backs.)

CARMELITA

Tacky shoes. No wonder they stuck you in the tank.

RODESIA

What tank?

CARMELITA

The tank is where they stick you when you break the dress code, and then they flash slides of chusmas in chusma outfits. Every time a slide comes on they whisper . . .

DESIREE

Shame.

Throughout Carmelita's speech, Desiree will cry "Shame" repeatedly, her voice getting louder until, at the end of the speech, she is hysterical.

CARMELITA

Every time a slide comes on, the voices whisper "Shame." And the voices get louder and louder and the slides go faster and faster. There are slides of chusma men, with bellies in tank tops with big gold medallions, drinking beer from cans. And chusma men and women smiling with their gold teeth. And chusmas that don't know how to match their outfits—floral prints with stripes. And even ancestral chusma women in housedresses with big fat foamy haircurlers going to the corner bodega for a pack of Marlboros and pork chuletas in chancletas.

Desiree, in a fit of hysterics, falls back on the table and rocks herself. Rodesia, who has been nodding throughout, now snores. Carmelita goes to comfort Desiree.

CARMELITA

There, there, Desiree. You'll be all right.

DESIREE

I can't take it anymore. I still have three months. I want it over. I want these months over already.

CARMELITA

In three months Rodesia will be transferred from this facility. She's failed every class, including Perfume Appreciation. She can't tell Chanel Number 5 from Agua de Florida Toilette Water. The doctors want her in intensive rehab. (She strokes Rodesia's hair.) Mi cielo, how peacefully you sleep. In the spring you will wake up and leave me. Desiree, you want to speed up time. I want time to stop.

Desiree's back is on the table and when she lifts her legs a sign with the number 12 drops down on and hangs above them. Desiree's legs simulate the hands of a clock, her shoes have arrows painted on the soles. Her legs move clockwise as music comes on. Carmelita dances and tries to stop her legs from keeping time, making them go counterclockwise. Carmelita translates the song, "Reloj," a Latin standard.

CARMELITA

Oh, clock don't mark the hours, or I'll go crazy. She will leave me forever when the morning comes and we only have tonight to live our love. (She holds on to Desiree's legs, sobbing.)

Scene 10

In Carmelita's cell at The BMU. Carmelita is enjoying an orgasmic pill while Rodesia, who dropped hers on the floor, is looking for it.

CARMELITA

Ah, ah, ahh.

RODESIA

Wait, I dropped my pill.

CARMELITA

(Letting out a big squeal) Ahh.

RODESIA

The door . . . (She goes to the door, which has opened. She checks to see if anyone there.) Strange, that keeps happening. That's the fifth time it's opened.

CARMELITA

Oh, more than that.

RODESIA

What do you mean?

CARMELITA

Whenever I'm in my cubicle for my classes, Accent Reduction, Conflict Resolution in Modulated Tones, The History of the DAR, I start to fall asleep so I pop a pill and . . .

RODESIA

(Cutting her off) You take that many pills?

CARMELITA

They're addictive. They got the nicotine. It's a come and perk, two in one.

RODESIA

And the door opens without the guard?

CARMELITA

Yeah.

RODESIA

When you're with me or you are alone, the door opens. What are the other denominators, what are the other conditions for this causality?

CARMELITA

Me in the room, or in the cubicle . . .

RODESIA

Yes, you said that. You taking the pleasure pill. BMU doors operate on an electromagnetic field. (Growling) Damn, this is where a science class would have come in handy. I can't tell you how many times I've asked for it and been denied.

CARMELITA

Wait. Last semester I took advanced housecleaning. There was chemistry and physics. Oh, what was that chapter on vacuuming hazards? Come on, chusma brain. A high-pitched sound of twenty-five nano-megahertz can create a disturbance in the electromagnetic field which can result in vacuum cleaners expelling instead of sucking, and doors operating on an electromagnetic field to open. A high-pitched sound of twenty-five nano-megahertz?

RODESIA

Like a high-pitched squeal!

CARMELITA

(Upset, goes to sit down) Maybe.

RODESIA

Oh, honey, I love that sound. I love it. But you know what this means?

CARMELITA

(Haughty but clueless) Of course.

RODESIA

Escape.

CARMELITA

Escape!

RODESIA

Tomorrow will be perfect. Everyone will be celebrating in the big hall. There'll be so many distractions, noise . . . (She notices Carmelita is sad.) What's the matter?

CARMELITA

If this is true and we're gonna escape, I'm thinking of Desiree.

RODESIA

No one could help her, not even you. Too many months in solitary refinement. She finally broke. But there's still us. Will you come with me?

CARMELITA

What a question. I've been here for thirteen miserable years, rottin' in this hellhole. My life has been snuffed out. I'm an artist. I got a couple of more swan songs left in me yet. (Highly dramatic) I want to live, live.

RODESIA

Freedom. Can you feel the snowfall, smell the skunk? I'll teach you spelunking. We'll go to the mountains.

CARMELITA

Spelunking! (Excited) Oh, I've always wanted to play the Catskills.

RODESIA

I was thinking of the Rockies.

CARMELITA

How about a Lincoln Log cabin with bidet. Maybe I'll open up a canteen and have shows.

RODESIA

Where we're going there'll be no people. Just me and you in the wilds.

CARMELITA

You talk like an ancient lesbian separatist.

RODESIA

The world sucks. Look at the world. One huge mall. Kids with guns. You gotta be a billionaire to become president. Some people are legal, some not.

CARMELITA

Like my clones.

RODESIA

Yeah. And look at all the antihumani prejudice there is. A woman can be with another woman and that's okay, but a chusma woman like you and a woman-oso humani like me, we couldn't holds hands together or kiss in public. You know how many humani epithets we'd get. I'd have to hide my fur so I wouldn't hear construction workers yelling: "Hey Joe, get a load of that humani, check out the fur." I can't take that bashing anymore. Nope. Where I'm going I'll be praying in the cathedrals of evergreens, swimming in an icy-cold glacial lake, and slurping on some honey at the Honeycomb Canteen with a couple bees. Want to come?

CARMELITA

Of course.

Scene 11

At the BMU by a door. Carmelita and Rodesia are about to escape. Sounds associated with New Year's Eve are heard: noisemakers, whistles, etc. Carmelita hands Rodesia a large cup.

CARMELITA

Come on, you have to drink it all. You have to stay up past midnight.

RODESIA

There's no milk.

CARMELITA

It's stronger that way.

RODESIA

It smells burnt.

CARMELITA

It's Starbucks. They bought everyone out. El Pico, Chock Full o' Nuts. Do you remember: Chock Full of Nuts is the heavenly coffee, heavenly coffee?

RODESIA

No.

CARMELITA

What about: En mi casa toman Bustelo, en mi casa toman Bustelo . . .

RODESIA

No.

CARMELITA

You gotta know this one. Celebrate the moments of your life . . .

RODESIA

No.

CARMELITA

What a world we have created. One megamonopoly of a corporation. There's only one coffee: Starbucks and one mall: Kmart.

Rodesia drinks the coffee as Carmelita fixes her hair. The coffee has a quick effect on Rodesia.

RODESIA

My heart. Wow. . . . Come on . . . Take your pill, pill, pill. (shaking)

CARMELITA

Wow, I never saw anyone get such a quick fix. (She takes her pill and starts moaning.) **Ah, ah.**

The offstage voice of a radio announcer is heard.

RADIO DJ

Hello, inmates throughout the metropolitan BMUs. This is, you guessed it, Bobbie from WQXR. Ready for the countdown. Ten, nine, eight, seven . . .

Carmelita comes with a squeal and the door opens. They exit offstage and we hear them, but don't see them, while the countdown continues.

RODESIA

Come on, come on, other pill, come . . .

CARMELITA

Shit, you made me drop my pill.

RODESIA

(Agitated) **No time, guard's coming . . .**

RADIO DJ

Six, five, . . .

RODESIA

Come manually, the natural way . . .

CARMELITA

Ah, ah, ah . . .

RADIO DJ

Four, three, two, one . . .

CARMELITA

(Lets out a squeal.) **Ah.**

RADIO DJ

Happy 2013, everybody.

RODESIA

(Yelling) Run, baby, run.

Scene 12

Eerie music is heard. The Free Zone, a deserted space with lighting that suggests radioactive waste. There is a curtain made of neon-orange plastic mesh used in temporary construction sites. There are plastic yellow warning signs and flowers. Rodesia comes in, dragging a tired Carmelita, and sets her down by a bench. She walks through the Free Zone.

RODESIA

We made it. It's the Free Zone. Nothing grows, everything glows. Look at that moon. Smell the air, acid rain, and cow manure. Look at that cow. (Carmelita lies down and falls asleep.) Say, maybe you'd like to teach me how to do it the natural way. I'll show you my fur. (She sees that Carmelita has fallen asleep and is talking in her sleep. She goes to her.)

CARMELITA

I ain't got no bail, got out of jail, but I'm hungry like the wolf . . . doo . . . doo.

Rodesia caresses her and takes out a pencil and paper and writes her a note. She places it in Carmelita's pocket, kisses her, and exits sadly. Lights get brighter, suggesting the morning, as Carmelita wakes up and stretches.

CARMELITA

I needed that. Ro. Where are you? Looking for berries? (She gets up and realizes Rodesia has left her. She feels the letter in pocket and reads it.) Darling. I saw you singing and dancing with wolves last night and know we must part for a little while. You have a song in your heart, I have a mountain in mine. Look for me in the Rockies, coordinates five west, ten south, latitude thirty-five across from Medicine Hat. I'll be building you a log cabin with bidet for you and your clones. Every summer I'll be waiting.

Para siempre tu woman-oso, Ro. P.S.: I'm leaving you this ring for our commitment ceremony. Oh my God (crying), it's got a little fur from her lower back. Oh Ro. (sobbing)

Scene 13

In the dark an offstage newscast announcement is heard.

ANNOUNCER

This just in from the FBI's DNA BMU. Two illegal clones have escaped their respective BMUs. Clana Balboa escaped Miami's 8th Street BMU; Cluna Bilboa has escaped the South Bronx BMU. Should you see these individuals, be careful: they carry the chusma gene. They may be dangerous and rude. Back to you, Bobbie.

At the Free Zone. B-movie music comes on as Clana and Cluna, Carmelita's clones, dance a stylized escape. They go in opposite directions, missing one another. Clana does cartwheels. Each crosses the stage individually until they bump into each other in the middle.

CLUNA

Coño, chica.

CLANA

Coño yourself.

CLUNA

Oh, yeah, girl (threatening).

CLANA

Yeah (with attitude).

They stare at each other and realize something's up. Clana walks around Cluna and stares at her.

CLUNA

You (mesmerized).

CLANA

(Mesmerized) You.

CLUNA

Beautiful eyes.

CLANA

Beautiful mouth.

CLUNA

What a fox!

CLANA

Like staring at my reflection in a toilet bowl full of clean water.

CLUNA

Spitting image.

CLANA

Where are you from, girl?

CLUNA

The Bronx, France. Je parle Français. And you?

CLANA

Miami, Cuba. Mucho Spanglish.

CLUNA

Did you see the Army Corps of Engineers dragging the island and attaching it to the coast of Miami?

CLANA

Only on TV. (A siren is heard offstage.) There's a cave over there, run this way. (Schtick.)

They sit down and a plastic bat is thrown at them.

CLUNA

Oh, I love caves with bats. My favorite pets are rats and bats.

CLANA

Me, too. I wanted them as pets but the unit manager—I mean my father.

CLUNA

Relax sister. You're safe with me. (She flings the bat to the other side of the stage.) Moi et vous, in this cave, c'est toute.

CLANA

I feel very connected, like we had to meet.

CLUNA

We're two peas in a pod.

CLANA

Corta' por la misma tijera.

CLUNA

I bet your name is like mine. It begins with two letters: *C* and *L*.

CLANA

Yes. Clana, and you?

CLUNA

Cluna.

CLANA

Oh, let me see. Come on. (Cluna turns around as Clana pulls down her pants and reads the information that is written on her butt.) CL illegal. Year 2000. One of two. Bio-original: CT, Lower East Side Performance Artist-Chusma. Check mine out.

CLUNA

I don't have to. I see the same exact butt.

CLANA

I want you to. (She turns around as Cluna pulls down her pants and reads.)

CLUNA

Same year, same make, same bio-original. We're twin clones.

CLANA

Coño.

CLUNA

Coño is right.

CLANA

That's a forbidden word.

CLUNA

(Bitterly) Well, lot's of things are forbidden, especially when you are an illegal clone and your bio-original was a chusma. It's like we never even had a chance. It makes me mad.

CLANA

Me, too.

CLUNA

As a kid I was always told "Control that gene, Cluna."

CLANA

Me, too. People used to say (with a refined American accent) "Clana, don't be like your original, behave." Behave. I tried, but always something would happen when I least expected it. I was programmed to be a ballerina. I apprenticed and got to be understudy for Alicia Alonso's clone CL-Alicia. She got sick and I had to go on for her. It was *Swan Lake*. (She begins to dance ballet, carried by the memory. A music-box tune is heard.) I danced for fifteen minutes and all was perfect, and then I don't know what happened. (She switches from ballet to wild Latin, as if possessed by the spirit, and the soft music turns to fast mambo.) I just heard this music in my head, and it was too much for me. I just let her rip. (She stops dancing and composes herself.) They told me I had to go to rehab. I got mad and escaped.

CLUNA

Girl, you should have gotten a standing ovation for that pelvic action. They're crazy putting you in a unit.

CLANA

Cluna, do you ever wonder about our bio-original?

CLUNA

Every day. I think, Why did she make us knowing we'd be illegal? And who is she, anyway? And what the hell is a performance artist? And where's the Lower East Side? I have a million and one questions.

CLANA

When I can't sleep at night I just rub my butt where it says CT bio-original, and then I just go to sleep. Do you think we'll ever meet her?

CLUNA

Well, we met, didn't we?

CLANA

Yeah, but I've always wanted to meet my bio-original.

CLUNA

There's nothing stopping us. It could be our mission. That's what I've been missing: a mission.

CLANA

Me too. A mission.

CLUNA

Yeah.

CLANA

Our mission. Let's do it.

CLUNA

Yeah, but we'll start tomorrow, first let's catch some *z*'s before the sun's up.

They sit and put their arms around each other's necks.

CLANA

Good night, Cluna.

CLUNA

Good night, Clana.

Scene 14

The Free Zone. Carmelita, lost, tries to find her way. She walks aimlessly in a dress made out of green plastic sandwich wrap.

CARMELITA

Nothing but styrofoam and plastic. Sure, you can create an outfit and look great, but you can't eat plastic. (Looking out in the distance.) Oh my

God, is that, give me your poor, tired, and huddled masses Lady Liberty? (Police siren is heard.) Coast Guard Patrol. I'll wait till nightfall in my green outfit. I will look like a fish swimming ashore.

Scene 15

In a cave in the Free Zone. Cluna and Clana are wearing hats and sunglasses.

CLANA

What a day!

CLUNA

You said it sister. ¡Qué día!

CLANA

No one would recognize you with that hat.

CLUNA

Or you. Estás requete bién. Y yo?

CLANA

Requete bón, chica.

They bump hips and laugh loudly.

CLUNA & CLANA

Bon chica, bon chica, bon bon.

CLUNA

Girl, didn't anybody tell you not to laugh like that?

CLANA

All the time.

CLUNA

Now we are free. We can laugh however.

CLANA

I can't believe we stole I.D.'s and hats.

CLUNA

Our mission depended on stealing I.D.'s and hats. The ends justify the means. Nothing matters. I took Marxism and existential French philosophy. French is very big in the Bronx. We have French kissing, French dressing, French fries.

CLANA

We are so alike, but different.

CLUNA

They developed my brain and expect me to get with their program—wrong.

CLANA

They developed my body and expect me to follow in their Ballet Russe rhythms—wrong.

CLUNA

We had to steal I.D.'s. No I.D.'s: no data bank info. So tell me Jane Hathaway . . . (She reads Clana's I.D. name.)

CLANA

Yes, Connie Chung.

CLUNA

What's the info on performance art?

CLANA

(Reading from a computer printout) Performance art. See Duchamp. See Dada. See performance art. Huh? I don't get it. What did you get?

CLUNA

(Reading from her own printout) Lower East Side. Obsolete term used before the new millennium for area in lower Manhattan. In the year 2000 numerous changes took place. The Bowery became Bouvier Boulevard and luxury housing developed up to Adelaide Boulevard, formerly known as Avenue A. Left of that the landfilled East River was designated Chusmatown. Chusmatown is where the highest concentration of the city's Chusmas live and work. There are legal industries like shoe factories as well as illegal ones.

CLANA

Chusmatown.

CLUNA

We have to go Chusmatown.

CLANA

I'm scared.

CLUNA

Don't be.

CLANA

I got nervous when we had to go and use different computers. I don't like to get separated.

CLUNA

We won't get separated.

CLANA

What if I have to do number one?

CLUNA

I'll go with you.

CLANA

And number two?

CLUNA

Number one, two, or three. Together.

CLANA & CLUNA

Codependent forever!

Scene 16

The streets of Chusmatown. Carmelita walks the streets of Chusmatown in a skimpy outfit.

CARMELITA

Oh, woe is me. They think I'm a ho. I'm just an honest chusma trying to make six hundred dollars an hour minimum wage windshield washing along the FDR Drive to prevent road rage. Motorists no longer want to kill one another because a chusma with a rag and a smile will defuse aggresivity. They paw us, they call us names. Chusmatown is no picnic for us illegal Chusmas. It's been a year that I've been living hand-to-mouth, always on the run from the Chusma police. Estoy desesperada. My only hope is to get legalization papers. (Kneeling down in prayer) Forgive me Virgencita for what I am about to do. I know I swore to you no more violence, but I need papers. And there's only one place to get them. I could get killed. (Getting up) Hell, if I die, at least I'll die in the limelight.

Scene 17

The streets of Chusmatown. Clana and Cluna sit on a bench disguised in hats.

CLANA

My eyes hurt.

CLUNA

Well, lower your veil. Even the ozone hole is bigger in Chusmatown. (Cluna takes the last bite of a candy bar and Clana hits her.)

CLANA

Hey, that was the last bite.

CLUNA

Yeah.

CLANA

It was mine.

CLUNA

Oh, yeah, girl.

CLANA

Yeah. Don't go telling me what to do.

Carmelita, wearing a Mexican wrestling mask and carrying a little banana in her hand, crosses the stage, jogging. She then stretches and practices a couple of martial arts kicks. Clana and Cluna do not pay attention to her.

CLUNA

Why not? I'm the brain.

CLANA

Big brain, look where we are, Chusmatown. No one wants to hire Jane Hathaway and Connie Chung. And every time we ask anyone about performance art, they look at us as if we are from Uranus. It's mission impossible.

Carmelita notices them and gets closer.

CLUNA

Oh, yeah. Well maybe our bio-original is not the fairy princess you think. She gave us up. She doesn't care we are broke, hungry, and en chômage without fromage.

CLANA

Speak English!

CLUNA

Unemployed without cheddar, dammit.

They face each other as if about to hit each other. Carmelita goes to stop the fight and sits with them.

CARMELITA

Hey, hey, girls. Stop the conflict. Figure out needs and negotiate. What happened?

CLUNA

She blames me because she's hungry.

CLANA

You ate the last bite.

CLUNA

No, I didn't.

CARMELITA

Silence. You are lucky. I always carry a candy bar or fruit with me to give to someone more down and out than myself. Are you two sisters?

Clana and Cluna don't know what to say and look at each other. Carmelita takes the banana she carries and hands a piece to Clana and a piece to Cluna.

CLUNA

Yeah.

CARMELITA

Always share. Here.

CLUNA

I don't want any.

CARMELITA

Yes, you do. You remind me of myself as a teenager. Come on. (Cluna takes the banana.) You are lucky to have one another. I have no one.

CLUNA

No one?

CLANA

But, you're so nice.

CARMELITA

I know. (She gets up and sings the dialogue a capella as if it were an opera.) Everyone has been taken away from me. My lover and I were separated, and my two, two clo . . . (overcome by emotion, she doesn't finish the word *clone*, and breaks down in sobs) baby, baby were wrenched from my bosom as babies. (She stops the operatic singing, becoming self-conscious, and goes to sit down by them.) I'm sorry. There's a lot of stress in Chusmatown. Are you two Chusmas? (Clana and Cluna look at each other and don't answer.) That's all right. You don't have to tell me. I'm just a stranger in a strange mask.

The important thing is that you are true to yourselves. Wear no mask when you look at yourself in the mirror. If you do, you won't see your face. And two sisters, dos hermanitas. Look out for one another. (She exits, walking very chusma.)

CLUNA

What a chusma!

CLANA

I feel strange.

CLUNA

Me too. A stranger in a mask gives us wisdom: Wear no mask when you look at yourself in the mirror, and a banana.

CLANA

It was like magic, but real.

CLUNA

Magic realism.

They look at each other, realizing they've been fighting.

CLANA & CLUNA

I'm sorry. I didn't mean it. No, I didn't.

CLUNA

We haven't taken our pills. So much anxiety. Not even an orgasmic pill to take off the edge.

CLANA

Estamos jodidas.

CLUNA

Not really. I've been thinking. There's one place we can go for our legalization papers.

CLANA

Where?

CLUNA

The Chusmatic Casino.

CLANA

It's illegal.

CLUNA

So are we. I hear it gets packed on Fridays with chusmas and well-dressed respectable nonchusmas. Their lives are so dull they gotta come for cheap chusma thrills. I read about it in the *Daily Chusma* while you were doing number three. Clana, with your physical ability and my mental strategy, we could do it. Without our papers, we're lost. We can't complete our mission. What do you say?

CLANA

It's mission posible.

Scene 18

The Chusmatic Casino. In the shadows, Dr. Igor, in a Mexican wrestling mask, is figuring out tomorrow's events and counting money.

DR. IGOR

What a match! Geraldo vs. Springer. Even at their age they still know how to fight. Eight billion euros, twenty-five million yen, thirty million dollars. At least my brain still computes.

Carmelita comes into the dark casino in her Mexican wrestling mask and trips.

CARMELITA

Coño.

DR. IGOR

Who's there?

A spotlight appears on stage and Carmelita steps into it.

CARMELITA

And God said: Let there be light and a spotlight appeared.

DR. IGOR

Pepe. Guard, guard . . .

CARMELITA

Please sir, madam, transgender, humani, whatever, please, I come for the auditions.

DR. IGOR

Too late.

CARMELITA

Please, you must give me a chance.

DR. IGOR

I got all the chusmas I need.

CARMELITA

Begging your pardon, you have chusma fakes and wannabes. You don't have the real McCoy chusma like me. In 1999 my TV show was terminated for its chusma content.

DR. IGOR

Who are you?

CARMELITA

Carmelita Tropicana, and the fates have conspired against me. I am a fugitive. And so bitter I will wrestle like no one else. Set an army against me and I will kill or be killed.

DR. IGOR

Name your prize: money, organs, or papers?

CARMELITA

Papers.

DR. IGOR

The fiercest opponents fight for papers. They are the bloodiest fights. Eyeballs are yanked from their sockets, limbs are severed, earlobes torn.

CARMELITA

I need my papers.

DR. IGOR

All right. Take the stairs to the cellar. There's a dressing room with a skull. And watch out for the rats.

CARMELITA

Rats, how nice. (She exits, leaving Dr. Igor alone.)

DR. IGOR

For fifteen years I waited and waited and waited. And now my wait is over. But who will I choose as her opponent? It has to be someone who can crush her and . . . Oh, my heart, my medicine . . . (Grabbing his heart, he falls on the floor.)

Clana and Cluna enter the Casino and don't notice him at first.

CLANA

I told you to hurry. We're probably too late now.

CLUNA

I had to do number three. (They see Dr. Igor.)

CLANA

Look. (Kneeling by him, they check him out.)

CLUNA

He looks like he had some kind of attack.

CLANA

You know CPR. Give him mouth-to-mouth.

CLUNA

I'll shake him first. Sir, monsieur.

CLANA

He's got a syringe.

CLUNA

Give me. (She injects him. He comes to immediately and stares first at Clana and then at Cluna.)

DR. IGOR

Oh, mon Dieu. Ce n'est pas possible. It's a dream, une rêve. Kick me, pinch me. (They pinch and kick.) Oh the pain, the joy. You are so strong. Help me up. (He takes them to the spotlight to look at them better.) Très jolie. Deux, sacrebleu coiffure.

CLUNA

Monsieur, we are here to audition for the chusma wrestling. Nous sommes chusma clones.

DR. IGOR

And you speak French.

CLUNA

I was in the Bronx for the French invasion. We want papers and we will fight our opponent to the bitter end.

DR. IGOR

And you?

CLANA

Of course. I was a student of Clachan.

DR. IGOR

Jackie Chan's clone, c'est magnifique. I have one opponent in mind. Looks can be deceiving. She is very powerful. It will be you two against one, you will have to take testosterone pills.

CLANA & CLUNA

We'll do anything for our papers.

DR. IGOR

That is what I want to hear. Take the elevator to the penthouse to the Dolly Parton dressing room. It's got a Jacuzzi.

CLUNA

Yes sir.

DR. IGOR

Call me papi. (He tries to grab her and she slaps his hand away.)

CLANA

Ai, papi.

DR. IGOR

I can't believe my eyes. This is so perfect. Revenge at last for Papa Chusma.

Scene 19

The Chusmatic Casino. Carnival music comes on as Dr. Igor, in a wrestling outfit with a cape, announces the fight.

DR. IGOR

Ladies and gentlemen. Welcome to the Chusmatic Casino. I am Papa Chusma, presenting the best in chusma wrestling. We have high-heel chusma, white chusmas, and senior citizen chusmas. But tonight we have the match of the millennium. We have a special treat for you tonight. Our contestants have been secluded in a soundproof booth. They do not know that the match today is between a bio-original and her two clones, but you do. Place your bets, ladies and gentlemen, for a crème de la crème match. Let the games begin with the chusma parade.

Carmelita, in a wrestling outfit with a Mexican mask, comes out and goes to the audience displaying her muscles. She is followed by Clana and Cluna, wearing similar outfits, who also interact with the audience.

DR. IGOR

Chusmas to the ring. (They all get into their corners.) In this corner, representing the Old World, we have La Gran Tirana. (Carmelita steps forward toward the crowd and bows to them, as Clana and Cluna boo her.) And in this corner, representing the New World Order, we have my personal favorites, Las Twin Brujas. (Carmelita boos them.) Because of the nature of the fight, should a contestant remove her mask, she will be disqualified and forfeit all prizes.

Carmelita ties her shoelace as the bell rings and Clana grabs her from behind. Carmelita elbows her and Clana staggers to her corner. Cluna circles and Carmelita pushes her away as Clana grabs her from behind, spins her, and throws her backwards onto

Cluna's back. Carmelita is lifted up and with her legs up in the air is thrown onto Clana, who throws her down. As Carmelita stumbles backwards Cluna grabs her arms and Clana her legs. They have swung her several times when Clana realizes Carmelita is the lady that gave them the banana.

CLANA

Hey isn't this the nice lady that gave us the fruit?

CLUNA

No, her mask was red. (They stop swinging her and Clana drops her legs.)

CLANA

I'm sure she's the lady that gave us fruit. I'm sorry, but I cannot hurt a nice chusma. I forfeit. (Clana takes off her mask and Carmelita looks at her.)

CARMELITA

Like staring at my reflection in a toilet bowl full of clean water. (Carmelita takes off her mask.)

CARMELITA

I forfeit also.

CLANA

My bio.

CLUNA

(Taking off her mask) **Our bio.**

All three hold hands lovingly.

CARMELITA

(Overcome with emotion) **My clones.**

DR. IGOR

(Taking off his mask) **They are my clones.**

CARMELITA

Dr. Igor!

DR. IGOR

The man you laser stun-gunned.

CARMELITA

I thought you were . . .

DR. IGOR

Dead? Because of you I'm a shell of a man. My mind is not the same. I had to give up science, my laboratory. And my legs, I can no longer enjoy walks around the aisles of the supermarket.

CARMELITA

I'm sorry, but I paid for that unfortunate accident. I had to protect my babies.

DR. IGOR

Protect? You never wanted them.

CLUNA

Is that true?

CARMELITA

The truth is I never wanted to bring illegal clones into the world knowing they would have no opportunities, but the moment I held you . . .

DR. IGOR

I held them first. And sang to them. They would have had opportunities with me.

CARMELITA

You, you injected them with hormones so they'd grow faster, put makeup on them when they couldn't even walk. You are a selfish, sick scientist. You abused science for your own personal fantasy. Look at these girls: They have never known freedom. Maybe it's time they tasted it. Even though they are only fourteen years old with very mature bodies, I think they are ready to exercise their civil clone liberties. Let them choose who they will live with.

DR. IGOR

Agreed. Girls, I am your papa, the man who cloned you. I built this casino for you. You will have papers, and more. My empire is yours. (He bows to Carmelita.) Mademoiselle.

CARMELITA

Girls, I am an artist. I ain't got a pot to piss in. With me you'll inherit the wind, but we can be family. And there is a woman I would like you to meet, a woman with a heart of bear.

CLANA

You're my bio.

CLUNA

Our bio.

CARMELITA

Out of the mouth of babes. There is hope after all. Look at us, we are all in the soup together. All complicit in this Chusmatic Casino. You, Igor, for pitting chusma against chusma, we chusmas for fighting one another, and you ladies and gentlemen for coming here to watch chusmas degrade themselves before your very eyes. Well, we have our dignity. We are proud of our bodies, our accents, our emotions. Igor, always a wanna-be chusma. It's time you accepted yourself for who you are. Sit and we'll dedicate to you this dernier cri from a woman who gave us not Dada but mama art, a woman who made the magic real for little boys who dreamed of one day wearing eyelashes, sequins, and mascara, the one and only La Lupe.

A tape of La Lupe singing "This Is My Life" comes on as Carmelita, Clana, and Cluna dance and sing the song.

CARMELITA

Funny how a lonely day can make a person say,
What good is my life?

CLUNA

Funny how an aching heart can make me stop to say,
What good is my life?

CLANA

Still I look around and see this great big thing is
part of me and my life.

CARMELITA

This is my life today. Tomorrow love will come
and find me.

CLANA & CLUNA

For that's the way that I was brought to be.

Carmelita turns, showing her butt to the audience, and Clana and Cluna point to her butt.

ALL

This is me, this is me.

Carmelita points to them and they point to her.

This is my life and I don't give a damn for lost emotions.
It's such a lot of love I got to give. Let me live, let me live.

They scratch themselves and pull their hair like La Lupe used to do when singing.

CARMELITA

Sometimes when I feel afraid I think of what a mess
I made of my life.

CLANA

Crying over my mistakes, forgetting all the breaks
I had in my life.

CLUNA

I was put on earth to be a part of this great thing,
it's me, it's my life.

ALL

Guess I will just have to score and count the things
I'm grateful for in my life.

CARMELITA

This is my life today. Tomorrow love will come and find me.

CLANA & CLUNA

For that's the way that I was brought to be, this is me.

CARMELITA

This is me.

ALL

This is my life and I don't give a damn for lost emotions.
There's such a lot of love I got to give, let me live, please.

All kneel down.

Let me live.

CLANA

This is my life.

Cluna goes in front of Clana.

CLUNA

This is my life.

CARMELITA

(Crawls from under their legs, gets in front of them both and belts out)
This is my life.

The End

Sor Juana: The Nightmare

A work in progress by Carmelita Tropicana and Ela Troyano

This work is based on the life of Sor Juana Inés de la Cruz, a seventeenth-century Mexican nun who wrote poetry, plays, and songs.

Cast

Sor Juana, a tough, smart, self-educated nun

Vicereine, a patron of the arts; a rich, powerful aristocrat

Alba, Sor Juana's slave/servant, poor, uneducated but smart, who will become Prosecutor's Aide in the dream

Prosecutor/Archbishop, a religious zealot

Time

Seventeenth-century Mexico

Setting

The Vicereine and Sor Juana are in the convent locutory, a place where nuns can receive visitors. Bars or metal grille separate the nuns from their visitors.

Because it is a dream, the bars have now been transformed into a spider's web. Juana is asleep, sitting on a chair opposite the Vicereine. She has fallen asleep with a pen in hand and has papers on her lap. The Vicereine has a dress with a belt made of plastic which holds water and plastic fish.

VICEREINE

Juana. (Juana opens her eyes.) I will call you plain Juana today.

JUANA

Your Excellency. (Surprised) You are here today. Your dress: Does it have fish?

VICEREINE

Yes, Juana. I'm full of life. Sea life. I want to show you what's out there. Put away your writing and come with me tonight.

JUANA

Your Excellency, I cannot leave the convent. I'm a nun. I've made my vows: obedience, poverty, chastity, and enclosure. I'm cloistered for life.

VICEREINE

It's only for one night. If you come, I promise to publish all your work. All of it, if you come.

JUANA

I'm so grateful to Your Excellency. But I don't think I can; I am bound.

VICEREINE

Juana, you're a poet. A rara avis. A rare bird cannot be jailed forever. Even a bird can fly out for one night. You can take the poem with you. A writer needs to see things with her own eyes, without bars to cloud her vision.

JUANA

I don't know. They are not going to let me out.

VICEREINE

Look up. (A hanger is lowered with a cape, hat, and sword that resemble the outfits of the Three Musketeers. Juana holds the disguise lovingly.) Put it on. You have to take off your habit. (She turns her back on Juana and, when Juana is busy dressing, turns to look at her lasciviously.)

JUANA

(As she's dressing) Without the skirt I can run. With the cape I can fly. A predator, an eagle. The wings close to the body. I open my wings and I'm ready to hunt. I'll trade my veil for a hat. Both hide one of man's greatest temptations: a woman's curls. When it's long, cascading down the nape of the neck, a weapon as lethal as a sword. (She holds her sword.) The final piece. I'm ready for anything, Your Excellency. (As she says the last words, Alba, her slave, enters, dressed as the Egyptian goddess Isis.)

ALBA

What are you doing, Juana?

JUANA

You recognized me.

ALBA

I know you better than you know yourself. You'd better listen.

JUANA

(Shocked at Alba's tone) Alba!

ALBA

Someone has to talk sense into you. She's putting crazy ideas in your head.

JUANA

She wants one night.

ALBA

There'll be trouble.

JUANA

I have this (raises her sword).

ALBA

Men use swords. A woman uses her head.

VICEREINE

You've given your slave too much slack. Time to tighten the rope.

ALBA

Don't go.

VICEREINE

I am María Luisa . . . Countess de Paredes.

ALBA

She'll leave you. I won't. I belong to you. I'm your slave.

VICEREINE

Juana, you said you were my slave.

ALBA

She can't take care of you like I can.

JUANA

I will see the sky with my eyes. There'll be no bars.

ALBA

That's my Juana. More eyes than a peacock. Always looking. A woman of many disguises. Be careful with the sword; one day you will need it to slay the demons.

Juana takes the sword and is about to break the web. The Vicereine covers her ears, expecting to hear a crash. Alba holds Juana's hand with the sword to stop her.

ALBA

No, Juana. The sword is for demons. Give someone a sword and they want to use it for everything. (She takes hold of Juana's hands and shows her a spot where she can go through.) See? Sometimes freedom is easier than it looks.

Lights off Alba as she exits, leaving Juana for the first time face to face with the Vicereine.

VICEREINE

How do I look?

JUANA

Radiant.

VICEREINE

You look dashingly handsome. Señor Juan. You may kiss me now. (Juana kisses the Vicereine's hands over and over.) Are you finished being a gentleman? (Commanding her) The lips. (Juana hesitates) My husband kisses me on the lips.

JUANA

I may die of bliss.

VICEREINE

And I'll die waiting. (They kiss passionately until the sword gets in their way and the Vicereine starts to giggle.) Your sword, it's hard.

Church bells ring.

JUANA

Evening vespers. The nuns will be coming any moment to pray. Yesterday the wind was blowing. I saw the wind lift their veils and they turned into bats. Let's go before the bats come. (They walk out of the convent and a new set appears. It suggests heaven, earth, and an underwater landscape. A crab underwater is also part of the constellation Cancer. There are algae and fish.) My. Look at that sky. The world looks so different. It smells of eucalyptus. (They both stand and inhale.)

VICEREINE

And ocean brine.

JUANA

I've never seen or smelled the ocean.

VICEREINE

Let's rest. I'm tired. (She sits near a snake but doesn't see it.) Fetch me something to eat.

JUANA

(Looking around, examining things) A toad. What beautiful eyes, dry skin. I couldn't kill it. What is this? An ear? Of some animal. It smells smoky. It's a pig's ear. Look. (She's excited. The Vicereine couldn't care less.) If I hold it up to the light it shows tiny veins, little rivers that have stopped flowing. Isis says: "Él que nació lechón tiene que morir puerco."

VICEREINE

He who was born a pig must die a pork. (She starts to look for something to eat. She finds a cut onion and smells it. It makes her cry.)

JUANA

María Luisa, why are you crying?

VICEREINE

It's this. . . .

JUANA

My love. Your pain is my pain, your tears my tears. (She takes the onion and they both cry together.)

VICEREINE

Fetch me something wonderful to eat.

JUANA

I've always fed on beauty. (She sees a red rose and picks it. It is a chocolate rose wrapped in red foil. She brings it to the Vicereine and offers it to her, unwrapping it.) **I adore you. A rose is a rose. . . .**

VICEREINE

Eros c'est la vie. (Juana gives the rose to the Vicereine to taste.) **I'll always love you.** (The chocolate melts in Juana's hands as the Vicereine tastes it.) **So sweet.** (She looks at Juana's hand and screams.) **Juana, your hands! What are they: stigmata?**

JUANA

(Scared) **Stigmata?** (They are examining her hands when lights go up on the Prosecutor, wearing an executioner's mask and sitting in a tall chair.)

PROSECUTOR

In nomini patris, et filio, et spiritu sancto. Amen. Did I hear stigmata? I may be hard of hearing but some words pierce me. A piercing sound inaudible to anyone but me. I am Head Prosecutor for the Inquisition. Chief Verificator. Ora pro nobis peccator peccatoribus . . . (He prays while down below the Vicereine cowers, hiding.)

VICEREINE

(Whispering) **The Inquisition! God, Juana, I've seen what they do. They'll torture and kill us. You left the convent. I left my husband. Don't say who you are.**

JUANA

I won't. I'll protect you.

VICEREINE

Juana, it's the Inquisition.

PROSECUTOR

As Chief Verificator I have many tasks, but I specialize in stigmata, beatific visions, and virgin statues that cry human tears. Who are you?

JUANA

I am Juan de los Palotes. Good evening to you, Mister Prosecutor. I did not mean to disturb you.

PROSECUTOR

You are not disturbing me. When I hear stigmata called out it's my job to verify. I am a fisher of souls. (Taking a fishing rod and letting it down so it touches her hands.) Hold out your hands. Odd. Stigmata are red, bloody. I don't smell blood. It looks more like feces. And then stigmata appear mostly in women—nuns. Do you have a bit of lipstick on your mouth?

JUANA

I ate some berries.

PROSECUTOR

I distinctly heard stigmata. I don't have to tell you. . . . Are you Catholic?

JUANA

Yes sir. Of the one true, catholic, and apostolic Church.

PROSECUTOR

Make the sign of the cross.

JUANA

In the name of the mother, daughter . . . I didn't mean that, sir.

PROSECUTOR

Show me your cross.

JUANA

(She takes out her cross, but instead it's an Egyptian ankh. She tries to shape it into a cross.) I don't understand how this got here.

PROSECUTOR

Lick your stigma. (Juana does and it disappears.) An Egyptian ankh: a symbol of a barbaric people. A stigmata that vanishes. This could have serious consequences. Ora pro nobis . . . (He prays and swings a church incense holder.)

VICEREINE

Juana, I have to go.

JUANA

I need you, María Luisa.

VICEREINE

I can't.

JUANA

Don't leave me.

VICEREINE

(As she is about to exit) I have a husband and child. I have to.

PROSECUTOR

Not so fast, María Luisa. I have to get to the bottom of this.

JUANA

Sir, I will comply if you let her go. I will answer.

PROSECUTOR

Such nobility. Taking amor into your own hands. Speaking of hands, I noticed a ring on your hand.

The snakelike rock that's part of the set moves. It is the Prosecutor's Aide. She gets up, catching Juana and Vicereine by surprise.

VICEREINE

It's the devil.

PROSECUTOR

She works for me. We have eyes and ears everywhere. Raise her hands. (The Prosecutor's Aide raises Juana's arms for inspection.) What's that other ring?

JUANA

It's a friendship ring. I gave it to her. It has her portrait painted on it.

PROSECUTOR

Her portrait. What vanity. A most detestable quality in a woman. (Screaming angrily) Who are you? I want the truth.

JUANA

Sor Juana Inés de la Cruz.

PROSECUTOR

The poet nun. The one everyone's been talking about. You criticized a sermon by Father Viera. Amazing. A nun criticizing a learned father's sermon. The ring shows disobedience to husband and mother.

JUANA

What do you mean?

PROSECUTOR

I thought you were smart. Have you forgotten you are a bride of Christ? By giving her a ring you betrayed your husband. Two rings make you a bigamist. And what about your Mother—the Church? You left her. You should be sucking at her bosom. (He uncovers his robe to show a large prosthetic breast.) I'll make you a pact. I let her go, if you cut off your allegiance to her.

JUANA

I'll do anything for her freedom.

VICEREINE

Juana . . .

PROSECUTOR

Take off her ring. (Juana tries but can't.)

JUANA

I can't, it's stuck.

PROSECUTOR

Try harder. I'm waiting. Tie her.

The Aide puts Juana in restraints so that she resembles Jesus on the cross. She then blindfolds the Vicereine and takes Juana's sword. She leads the Vicereine to a dark corner and cuts off her finger. Both Juana and the Vicereine scream in agony.

JUANA & VICEREINE

No . . . no.

The Prosecutor's Aide gives the Vicereine a rag to wrap around her hand. The Vicereine exits, running and screaming, with the bloody rag.

PROSECUTOR

One finger for freedom seems fair. This is the Church Militant. The most Holy Inquisition. Now then, Sor Juana Inés de la Cruz, you have gained fame and wealth. As a nun you have vowed poverty. What good is fame and wealth if you should lose your soul? I can show mercy if you show me true repentance. Deal?

JUANA

(Weary) Yes.

PROSECUTOR

Good. You have strayed from your Master. You need to find Him. Juana, go find Christ. (To the Aide) Release her. Go, go find Christ.

JUANA

(Disoriented, looking all around) Christ. Christ is God. God is everywhere. God is the center of the universe. That answer is too inclusive, too catholic and not catholic enough. God is light. Not concrete enough. He's a bit dense. (Spotting a narcissus) Narcissus. Maybe too personal, but it is my truth. (She picks it and holds it up to the Prosecutor.)

PROSECUTOR

A narcissus?

JUANA

The divine narcissus. God created man in his own image. Christ is both God and man. The divine narcissus represents Christ, and Echo is the Devil tempting Christ.

PROSECUTOR

Mixing the life of Christ with Greek mythology: highly suspect.

JUANA

Lucifer is in love with Christ. Just as Echo is in love with Narcissus.

PROSECUTOR

That's a queer notion.

JUANA

It's in the Bible.

PROSECUTOR

First you correct sermons; now you interpret the Bible. Narcissus is a flower.

JUANA

As an artist I use symbols, metaphors to represent Christ's teachings. I wanted something as beautiful as Narcissus to illuminate spirituality. I tried verses reminiscent of the Song of Solomon.

PROSECUTOR

The Song of Solomon. Hah. The Church is in charge of protecting its members. Even the Bible can be a source of temptation. Those verses are too sensous, may give people ideas. They are forbidden. Don't tell me you don't know that?

JUANA

Isis, Isis.

PROSECUTOR

Who are you calling?

JUANA

Isis, the goddess of wisdom.

PROSECUTOR

Isis, the goddess of wisdom. Didn't you write that mental faculties are female . . . that's . . .

JUANA

Wait, you don't understand. Isis is a word that comes from Hebrew Is. Is. Double man. Double male. Don't you understand?

PROSECUTOR

Oh, what intellect you possess. Maybe we should ship you to Spain. We have given them Mexican gold, now we should give them Mexican intellect. What better way than to give them our pride, our Mexican phoenix. (The Prosecutor's Aide puts a big brain that oozes liquid on Juana's head.) Let me be the first to applaud. Sor Juana Inés de la Cruz, writer of profane plays, verses, songs. (He touches the brain.) Look at her. Her brain is full of ideas. There's an idea oozing out. (He smells his fingers.) Let me see. Oh, yes. She will be turning over a new leaf. She's taking her writing in a new direction. She's to become a mystic.

JUANA

What? I'm not a mystic, what are you saying?

PROSECUTOR

You haven't tried. (To Aide) Tie her up. (Juana is placed in restraints once more.) A little flagellation is what you need. (Alba cracks a whip several times, as the Prosecutor behaves as if in ecstasy.) Oh, the sound of the whip is joy to my ears. I can feel welts rising up to God like the scent of fresh blood on walls, sheets. Nothing like it. Along with fasting, it will produce the most ecstatic visions. (Aide attaches the papers Juana has to the fishing rod and he takes them.) I failed to mention one of my other jobs. I am a writer. Or should I say I rewrite nuns' stories. I make their lives exemplary. I add a little Latin here, I add, I delete. I sign my name (looking through the papers, he tears some and lets some fall) . . . as biographer.

JUANA

No, no. My sword, I should have used my sword. Alba, where are you?

The Prosecutor's Aide takes off her snake's mask, revealing a saddened Alba.

ALBA

I'm here. Remember, Juana, dreams have meaning.

End of Nightmare

Screenplay

Carmelita Tropicana: Your Kunst Is Your Waffen

A film by and directed by Ela Troyano. Screenplay by Carmelita Tropicana and Ela Troyano. Full credits appear on page 195.

1. INTERIOR. THEATER CLUB. NIGHT.

Carmelita Tropicana, a low-rent Carmen Miranda dressed in a rainbow-colored tropical outfit, delivers a monologue.

CLOSE-UP of her face, hidden by a Spanish fan, which she lowers as she begins to speak to the camera.

CARMELITA

Hello people, you know me, I know you. I am Carmelita Tropicana. I say Loisaida is the place to be. It is multicultural, multinational, multigenerational, mucho multi. And like myself, you've got to be multilingual. I am very good with the tongue. As a matter of fact the first language I pick up when I come to New York is Jewish. I learn from my girlfriend Charo, she's Jewish. She teach me and I write poem for her in Jewish. I recite for you today. Title of the poem is "Oy Vey Number One." "Oy vey, I schlep and shlep, I hurt my tuchus today, I feel—meshuggener, oy vey." (Applause.) Danke, danke, danke.

2. EXTERIOR. STREET. LOWER EAST SIDE. NIGHT.

Police sirens are heard. TITLES are SUPERIMPOSED over Scene 2: "Carmelita Tropicana: Your Kunst Is Your Waffen. A film by Ela Troyano."

LONG SHOT of Carmelita walking home from a performance a couple of blocks away from her building. She is wearing a light coat resembling a cape and a boa, and carrying a bag. She passes a video store awash with blue light.

CLOSE-UP of her platform shoes walking on the pavement, then of a shadow on the ground. CLOSE-UP of sneakers following her. When she turns the corner, after passing a bus stop shelter, she turns, sensing something is up. At the door to her building, Carmelita fumbles with a large set of keys. The Mugger grabs her from behind and a struggle ensues.

MUGGER

Give me the money.

The Mugger, in a dirty hooded sweatshirt, attacks with a sharp object and, in the fight, Carmelita's coat is ripped. Carmelita, angrier now that her coat's been damaged, screams.

CARMELITA

My coat!

She lunges with fury at the attacker, who falls to the ground onto a pile of garbage bags. The Mugger remains on the ground.

Carmelita looks at a scratch on her wrist from the fight.

3. INTERIOR. CARMELITA'S BEDROOM. MORNING.

From her bedroom we see a street sign: Avenue C, Loisaida. On her bedroom wall is a movie poster of María Felix, a popular 1940s Mexican star, in a movie titled *La Estrella Vacía* (The Empty Star).

Through mosquito netting we see Carmelita, asleep. She stirs, knocking over a book entitled *Megalopolis* from her lap. Police sirens are heard, mixed with the sound of a telephone ringing. A rooster crows. Carmelita wakes up, startled.

The sound of police sirens, fire engines, boom boxes, and motorcycles punctuate the scene that follows, at times almost drowning out the conversations that are INTERCUT.

CARMELITA

(picking up the phone)

Hello.

4. INTERIOR.

CLOSE-UP of side of Dictator's face as she holds phone. She is a tough, middle-aged Chicana with a ganglike bandana on her forehead and blue sunglasses. Her thumb and index finger have long gold nails.

DICTATOR

Tropicana? Dictator. The five-borough action is set for high noon. You will be picked up by Orchidia at . . .

A click is heard.

3 (cont'd). INTERIOR OF CARMELITA'S BEDROOM. MORNING.

CARMELITA

Hold on, I have another call.

A click is heard again.

CARMELITA (cont'd)

(surprised)

¿Papi? ¿Qué es de tu vida?

SUBTITLE: Dad! Haven't seen you in years, what's up?

A car with a loud boom box passes outside. She covers her ear to block out the noise.

CARMELITA (cont'd)

Una sorpresa?

SUBTITLE: You have a surprise?

CARMELITA (cont'd)

(apprehensive)

Un hermanito. Aha. ¿Al hospital para qué? Cómo? Qué? De la prostata?

SUBTITLE: A little brother. To the hospital for what? . . . What? . . . Your prostate?

Fire engines are heard outside. The phone clicks again.

CARMELITA (cont'd)

Espérate un momento.

SUBTITLE: Hold on.

The phone clicks.

4 (cont'd). INTERIOR. MORNING.

CLOSE-UP of Dictator's full face.

DICTATOR

In the next ten years ten million children worldwide will be infected with AIDS; two-thirds of all the AIDS cases will be among women and children.

CLOSE-UP of Dictator's mouth.

DICTATOR (cont'd)

Do not put me on hold. I will see you at nine at Tompkins Square Park. Over.

3 (cont'd). INTERIOR. CARMELITA'S BEDROOM. MORNING.

Carmelita writes the information down on her hand, since she cannot find a piece of paper. She clicks the phone receiver again. Motorcycles pass by.

CARMELITA

Papi. Aha.

She writes down additional information on the other side of the same hand. We see the scratch from the night before. The information relates to the flight number and time of her brother's arrival.

CARMELITA (cont'd)

Papi. ¿Tienes teléfono donde llamarte?

SUBTITLE: Dad, do you have a telephone where I can reach you?

A tone is heard, as if the call were disconnected. Carmelita puts down the phone and looks at it. There is another phone call. The answering machine is heard picking up the call. Carmelita starts to slink slowly down on the bed. By the end of the phone message she has pulled the bed sheets over her head, as if dead.

WOMAN ON MACHINE

(a bit too sweet)

Hi, is this the super? This is Jane from upstairs. I don't have any hot water. Is there a problem with the boiler?

The conversation on the answering machine continues to be heard, repeatedly, as an echo from her mind: "boiler . . . boiler . . ."

5. EXTERIOR/INTERIOR. CARMELITA'S BUILDING. MORNING.

MEDIUM SHOT of Carmelita opening the metal door in the sidewalk that leads to the building's basement. She descends, in five-inch platform sneakers, flashlight in hand. Scary music and darkness set the mood as Carmelita follows her flashlight beam into the boiler room.

Boxes are strewn all around. She points her flashlight at the electric box on the wall and turns on the lights. CARMELITA'S POV: The boiler has been turned to OFF. She switches it to ON.

CARMELITA

(muttering)

¡Qué stupid jerk!

The loud roar of the boiler is heard as it comes on. CLOSE-UP of the boiler. Carmelita stands by the doorway. She hears a scratching sound coming from a box near the door. She points the flashlight at the box and sees a mouse in cartoon animation. The mouse, frightened, screams.

MOUSE

Eek!

CARMELITA

Ai!

Carmelita runs in one direction, the mouse in another.

6. EXTERIOR. CARMELITA'S BUILDING. MORNING.

ORCHIDIA, a pretty but spacy young Latina in black leather boots and jacket, stands ringing a doorbell. A palm tree with coconuts is painted on the door. No one answers. Looking up, she starts to yell.

ORCHIDIA

Carmelita! Carmelita!

She steps back from the door onto the sidewalk. She looks at her watch.

6-A. INTERIOR. CARMELITA'S BUILDING. MORNING.

CLOSE-UP of Carmelita's hands trying to open the basement door from the inside. She bangs on the door.

6-B. EXTERIOR. CARMELITA'S BUILDING. MORNING.

Orchidia looks around, not realizing that the banging is coming from below her. CLOSE-UP of Orchidia's feet. She realizes what is happening and steps off the metal entrance to the basement. Carmelita emerges, annoyed. She hands Orchidia a gold knapsack.

CARMELITA

(emerging through the door)

Qué space cadet. You're late. Dictator is going to kill us.

CLOSE-UP of Carmelita's hands closing the door. They walk.

ORCHIDIA

Ni siquiera hello. ¿Qué bicho te picó hoy?

SUBTITLE: You don't say hello; you don't give me a kiss. Did something bite you?

CARMELITA

I got mugged last night.

ORCHIDIA

Again!

CARMELITA

Third time!

ORCHIDIA

Wow. With a gun?

CARMELITA

I don't want to talk about it.

Orchidia steps in front of Carmelita and very genuinely hugs her. We see them in profile standing in front of a homestead building covered with posters of political action groups, including the Lesbian Avengers.

ORCHIDIA

I'm glad you're okay.

Carmelita pushes her away and continues to walk.

CARMELITA

Okay. Okay.

ORCHIDIA

Are you on a diet?

CARMELITA

So?

ORCHIDIA

(disappointed)

I got us bagels with cream cheese and walnuts.

CARMELITA

Stop torturing me! You're just like my father, calling to tell me I have an eight-year-old brother.

Carmelita starts jogging; Orchidia stands frozen.

ORCHIDIA

What?

Orchidia follows Carmelita. Camera catches them as they round the corner and Carmelita stretches her hand out to Orchidia in a give me gesture. Orchidia hands her a bagel. They do this without stopping. When they are in front of a casita, a makeshift house like those in the Caribbean built by neighborhood people on abandoned city lots, Carmelita stops for a second, breaks the bagel in pieces, and yells.

ORCHIDIA (cont'd)

Trump, Leona.

CLOSE-UP of ducks running out to eat the scattered bagel pieces.

7. EXTERIOR. STREET.

Mugger is washing by a fire hydrant as Carmelita and Orchidia pass by.

8. EXTERIOR. TOMPKINS SQUARE PARK.

The Twin Sisters, two lesbians with shaved heads wearing S-and-M black leather jackets and boots, wait with the Dictator, also dressed in a black leather jacket and boots. Dictator has a walkie-talkie.

WOMAN ON WALKIE-TALKIE (voice-over)

(through static)

Dictator, this is Lady Fingers from headquarters. Clinic is under attack. You must split up your troops. Can you hear me? Give me that jelly donut. . . .

DICTATOR

Headquarters, I hear you. Me and the twin sisters will cover Times Square. I'll send the space cadets to the mobilization site.

Carmelita and Orchidia enter frame. MEDIUM SHOT of Carmelita and Orchidia from behind. They stand at attention facing Dictator.

DICTATOR

You're late and missed your action. Lucky for you the clinic is under attack and in need of help. Go to the mobilization site. I'll see you there later.

DICTATOR (cont'd)

(nicely to the two girls)

Let's go, girls.

The two girls sneer and snap gum at Carmelita and Orchidia. Camera follows Dictator. Carmelita starts walking and Orchidia follows. They walk towards Third Street. We see them from behind: They are talking as they briskly walk.

Dictator and Two Girls run in military formation across the avenue. Carmelita and Orchidia do the same in the opposite direction and then turn around. Seeing Dictator in the distance, they both stop and raise their hands.

CARMELITA & ORCHIDIA

Taxi.

Sound of car brakes screeching to a halt is heard.

9. EXTERIOR. SOPHIA AT BUS STOP.

CLOSE-UP of "Do's and Don'ts" in a Hispanic magazine. SOPHIA, a dark-skinned Latina yuppie wanna-be, stands reading a magazine. She wears huge gold earrings.

SOPHIA (voice-over)

Don't wear big earrings. Gold knockers will not open corporate doors. CLOSE-UP of Sophia's mouth with fuchsia lipstick. She sighs. **Don't wear fuchsia fingernail polish with steak tartare lipstick.** CLOSE-UP of Sophia's face showing worried look. She checks her stocking. She sighs. **Experts agree that a barrier to Hispanic women achieving corporate success is none other than fashion.**

She picks up her briefcase and starts to walk.

10. EXTERIOR. ABORTION CLINIC. NOON.

MEDIUM SHOT of Carmelita and Orchidia linking arms with other women around them. Annette Jackson, a black TV news reporter with a shaved head, is standing by.

ANNETTE JACKSON

My news is this way?

Carmelita and Orchidia are still linked to the other women of the Defense Task Force. To the side stand Annette Jackson and a leader of the G.I.A., a women's political action group. The G.I.A. leader is a young white woman.

G.I.A. LEADER

(love struck)

Oh, Annette, I'm so glad you're here. I watch your show every week.

CARMELITA

I hate waiting. I almost wish they'd strike.

A leader in the defense action is wearing a hat and whistle and carries a walkie-talkie. She blows the whistle.

G.I.A. LEADER

(into walkie-talkie)

Alert. This is an alert. Here they come.

A group of three men are approaching. One is an Old Latino and the other two, young white men (Protesting Man #1 and Protesting Man #2). Carmelita and Orchidia's arms move in a wavelike motion, as if in struggle.

PROTESTING MAN #1

I pray for you, I pray for your soul.

PROTESTING MAN #2

You lezzi-commie baby-killers!

CLOSE-UP of Orchidia's legs. The Old Latino is between her legs, caressing and kissing them.

OLD LATINO

Qué piernotas.

SUBTITLE: What thick legs.

He kisses them.

OLD LATINO (cont'd)

Por la Virgen María.

SUBTITLE: Blessed be the Virgin Mary and all her saints.

ORCHIDIA

Viejo verde. Let go.

SUBTITLE: Off, you dirty old man.

She wiggles and tries to shake him off.

CLOSE-UP of Carmelita's legs. Another guy is between them. He is touching her and it tickles.

CARMELITA

(laughing)

Please, I beg. Don't.

CLOSE-UP of her face in agony, biting her lip.

11. INTERIOR. DELI ACROSS FROM ABORTION CLINIC. NOON.

Sophia is paying at the counter. The deli vendor is a typical gum-snapping Latina fly girl.

SOPHIA

Four ninety-nine for measly carrots? The Department of Consumer Affairs should check your scale.

VENDOR

Here's your change, thank you very much.

Sophia turns away.

VENDOR

Coño, ¡qué tacaña!

SUBTITLE: What a tightwad!

SOPHIA

¿Cómo? ¿Así es como tú tratas a tus customers?

SUBTITLE: What was that? Is this how you treat your customers?

VENDOR

Sorry, I didn't know you spoke Spanish.

SOPHIA

¿Y que tú crees que yo soy nena? ¿Una morena?

SUBTITLE: What, you think I'm black?

VENDOR

Sí, bueno, I'm not color blind. I thought you were black, okay?

SOPHIA

Well open up your eyes, honey, Latinas come in all different colors!

As Sophia leaves the deli she sees Carmelita and Orchidia entangled in the clinic defense mini-riot.

CLOSE-UP of Sophia's face. Her expression changes from that of a martyr to concern and a determination to save the day.

12. EXTERIOR. ABORTION CLINIC. NOON.

ANNETTE JACKSON

This is Annette Jackson reporting live from midtown Manhattan. All day today, members of G.I.A., a women's action organization, have been demonstrating throughout the city. Police have reported that over fifty members have been arrested. As you can see, I'm standing in front of this abortion clinic and as you can see . . .

One of the men bumps into her. A camera person is involved in the melee: shots of feet.

ANNETTE (cont'd)

it is being defended. . . .

There are sounds of a scuffle. PAN to linked arms and legs of some of the people defending the clinic, a woman in a wheelchair, and shots of the Protesting Men pushing and shoving to get into the clinic.

13. INTERIOR. JAIL. AFTERNOON.

Carmelita, Orchidia, and Sophia walk in single file as they enter the jail. The camera films them through prison bars.

SOPHIA

Siempre lo mismo. I always have to clean up your mess.

Carmelita enters first.

CARMELITA

Es que tú eres un anal retentive.

SOPHIA

Y tú un leech off society.

CARMELITA

Conspicuous consumer.

SOPHIA

Always having brunch in the middle of the afternoon. Get a job.

CARMELITA

I have a vision. A mission.

She raises her fist.

CARMELITA (cont'd)

I am a performance artiste.

Her hands are up, Olé style. They are now all inside the prison cell and the door slams shut very loudly. They are all silent as they confront their situation. They are all so self-involved that they fail to see a cot with a bundle on it in the corner of the cell.

Sophia turns to look at the bars.

SOPHIA

Why me?

CARMELITA

(to Orchidia)

It's always me. Never others.

SOPHIA

I'm your sister. I'm here because of you.

CARMELITA

I didn't invite you.

ORCHIDIA

Basta, you two.

SUBTITLE: Stop it.

Dee, the woman on the cot, lies in a fetal position. She coughs.

DEE

Shut up!

They look at her while Carmelita and Sophia continue their feud. They mirror each other, smoldering. Carmelita touches her hair; Sophia plays with her finely manicured nails. Orchidia is now touching the bars sensuously, as if they were something else. She's kind of dreamy. She's photographed in soft focus.

ORCHIDIA

I never imagined it like this.

She starts to put her hand in and out of the bars. Then she does the same thing with her feet. She starts to climb the bars and to hang from them.

ORCHIDIA (cont'd)

Ven, Carmelita.

SUBTITLE: Come, Carmelita.

CARMELITA

Otra vez con tu postmodern dance contact improv.

SUBTITLE: Again with your postmodern dance contact improv.

ORCHIDIA

Open yourself. Don't be so closed all the time.

Carmelita and Orchidia begin to move and climb, throwing themselves on the floor.

SOPHIA

(muttering ridicule)

You call that dancing? Parecen dos esquizofrénicas.

Their movements get wilder until Orchidia throws Carmelita onto the cot where she lands on Dee. Furious, Dee lets out a bloodcurdling scream.

DEE

Oooww! What the hell!

Carmelita recognizes her.

CLOSE-UP of Dee, Carmelita's mugger. She is white, poor, unkempt from being homeless, and sickly. But she is tough, jaded, with attitude.

CARMELITA

You're my mugger!!!

SOPHIA

Mugged? Police, help!

Dee gets up and approaches Carmelita. Carmelita goes over to Sophia, who is holding on to the bars, screaming.

CARMELITA

Sophia, please, you're gonna get us into trouble.

SOPHIA

Trouble? We're in jail. I haven't called my office. I went to lunch and disappeared.

Dee limps back to the cot. She is followed by a trail of blood. Carmelita points it out to Orchidia.

CLOSE-UP of blood on the floor.

ORCHIDIA

Necesita tampon.

SUBTITLE: She needs a tampon.

DEE

What?

She turns around, looks down, and lifts her shirt. She sees her bandage is leaking.

DEE (cont'd)

Damn.

CARMELITA

(sympathetically)

You want a doctor.

Dee continues her limping walk.

DEE

No doctors. No hospitals. They drug you.

SOPHIA

(snottily)

They drug you? Are you kidding? I would think you'd be happy.

Dee looks back at her.

DEE

Yeah. . . . If I could have my drug of choice. But last time they gave me this green stuff. I started seeing little green men. You don't know what they stick in you.

ORCHIDIA

She's right. I only go to holistic doctors. I'm a firm believer in the power of colonics.

Both Carmelita and Orchidia follow Dee to the cot. Dee sits down with her back resting against the wall. Carmelita and Orchidia sit on the space that is left.

SOPHIA

Van a coger una infección. No la toquen.

SUBTITLE: You're going to get infected. She's bloody. Don't touch her.

Orchidia looks around and senses that something is not right. She closes her eyes and sniffs as if she could better sense the space.

ORCHIDIA

I've got protection.

She takes a little plastic bag from her bra, holds it in front of her and stares at it.

CLOSE-UP of bag and then of Carmelita and Dee staring quizzically at it.

ORCHIDIA (cont'd)

Si un espíritu se te monta encima, pobre de ti.

CARMELITA

If an evil spirit climbs on you . . . once it's on you, you're jinxed.

Orchidia opens the bag and takes out powder. She sprinkles some on Carmelita, who lets her, and on Dee, who half-moves away. Orchidia gets up and offers some to Sophia.

ORCHIDIA

¿Quieres?

ORCHIDIA'S POV: Sophia is seen at an angle, near the bars.

SOPHIA

No thanks. I'd rather have a margarita.

She gets into the fantasy, wistfully savoring it.

SOPHIA (cont'd)

On the rocks, with salt.

She turns and we see the bars have made an imprint on her nice suit. Her hair is not as neat as it was when we first saw her at the bus stop. Throughout the jail scene she will appear more and more disheveled.

Orchidia moves to the center of the floor and sits in the lotus position. Carmelita is left with Dee. Both are sitting on the cot.

CARMELITA

I'm Carmelita, that's Orchidia, Sophia.

She waves to Sophia, hoping she will wave back, but Sophia doesn't respond. Carmelita turns to Dee.

CARMELITA (cont'd)

And you?

DEE

(looking at Carmelita menacingly)

Dee.

CARMELITA

Dee? . . . Dee? . . . Not Didi?

Dee glares at her.

CARMELITA (cont'd)

Well, Dee, I gotta tell you this, I don't think you should be mugging.

Dee spits on the floor. Carmelita is shocked at Dee's lack of manners.

CARMELITA (cont'd)

Ah! Don't spit! What if I want to take my shoes off?

Dee starts to punch her pillow and rearranges it.

CARMELITA (cont'd)

This is my first time here. You a regular?

Dee nods her head.

CARMELITA (cont'd)

What's it like?

Dee moves closer to Carmelita.

DEE

It's like a loud, bad, high-pitched subway car screech—a shriek before the car brakes.

CARMELITA

Does it brake?

DEE

For some. Don't brake for me, though. Maybe I got the evil spirit on me and I've been jinxed.

CARMELITA

I thought I was jinxed two years ago. The spirit climbed here.

She touches her left shoulder.

CARMELITA (cont'd)

My apartment burned down. Then it went here.

She touches her right shoulder.

CARMELITA (cont'd)

I crashed my car. Hit a drug dealer in a limo. And then it went here.

She holds her pinky up.

CARMELITA (cont'd)

I got my first commercial, broke my pinky . . . and couldn't play the stain that sings in the sink. I could have been a great stain.

She sighs. She takes off her shoe.

CARMELITA (cont'd)

Let's see what I got in the Cuban bank.

She takes out a five-dollar bill and places it next to Dee.

CARMELITA (cont'd)

Here.

SOPHIA

(appalled)

Are you giving a mugger money?

CARMELITA

She won't mug me again.

SOPHIA

She's a criminal.

Dee gives back the money.

DEE

Keep it.

(to Carmelita)

You're mental, but you—

(to Sophia)

You got a bad attitude.

Dee gets up to confront Sophia.

DEE (cont'd)

You'd like to wipe me out, wouldn't you? You're like every stinking person I know—my drunken father, the C.O., the goddamn pimp.

Dee walks toward Sophia. Sophia, undaunted, walks toward Dee. The two are seen in profile, CLOSE-UP.

SOPHIA

Did your father, pimp, or C.O. put the knife in your hand to mug her? Huh?

Carmelita gets in between them.

CARMELITA

It wasn't a knife.

SOPHIA

(yelling)

What, then?

CARMELITA

A Bic pen.

Dee, embarrassed, moves back some steps.

SOPHIA

A what?

ORCHIDIA

I can't concentrate; you're creating too much bad energy here.

SOPHIA

Dios mío, dos locas y una . . .

CARMELITA

Okay. Relax. ¿Por qué no cantas algo? Con la voz tan linda que tienes.

SUBTITLE: Okay. Relax. Why don't you sing something with that lovely voice of yours?

SOPHIA

Sing? We're in jail!

CARMELITA

(to Dee)

The gods played a horrible trick—they gave you, my sister, a beautiful voice and me the desire to sing.

Carmelita sings a scale.

A large waterbug makes its way to Orchidia's leg. Carmelita sees it, touches Dee's arm, and tries to warn Orchidia. She is petrified.

CARMELITA

Orchidia—

Carmelita screams.

CARMELITA (cont'd)

La cucaracha, la cucaracha on your thigh.

CLOSE-UP of Orchidia, frightened.

ORCHIDIA

Carmelita, quítamela, quítamela.

SUBTITLE: Take it off me, Carmelita, take it off me.

CLOSE-UP of Carmelita, distressed at her own cowardice.

CARMELITA

I can't.

Dee gets up confidently and slaps the bug away from her. The bug lands close to Sophia, who retreats to the bars. The bug continues toward Sophia. Dee follows the bug and steps on it.

There is a big crushing sound. Sophia is too proud to be grateful. They exchange glances. Dee makes her way back to the cot and Orchidia puts her hand on her arm.

ORCHIDIA

You were wonderful.

Carmelita shows a mixture of shame and jealousy. Dee cannot believe this bunch ended up in jail.

DEE

How did you guys get here?

CARMELITA

You know how sometimes something happens and you don't know what's happening as it's happening and then something happens that makes no sense?

DEE

(to Orchidia)

What did she say?

ORCHIDIA

(to Carmelita)

Vamos. Let's do it.

They both get in position to do G.I.A. chants and movements. As soon as they do, Sophia gets uneasy.

SOPHIA

(warning them)

If you do the one about the patriarchy I'll call the cops.

Carmelita and Orchidia begin chanting and doing choreographed movements.

ORCHIDIA

We belong to a women's organization.

(to Carmelita, getting into position)

We're here.

CARMELITA

Who's here?

CARMELITA & ORCHIDIA

G.I.A.

(spelling it out)

G-I-A

We're antisexist, antiracist
And very very lesbian and gay
In the fight Roe vs. Wade

CARMELITA

Eggs and ovaries

ORCHIDIA

Eggs and ovaries

CARMELITA & ORCHIDIA

They're mine. All mine.
And not the states'
Can't legislate
Uh, uhuh uh. Uh, uh, uh.
We'll win the fight for equal rights.

DEE

(to Sophia)

Dos locas.

SUBTITLE: Two nut cases.

SOPHIA

You're telling me.

ORCHIDIA

Wow. Hablas muy bien.

Orchidia and Carmelita go sit down on the cot and Dee moves to the side of the wall.

DEE

Poco.

SUBTITLE: A little.

I picked some up at Bedford. Upstate. I was doing time for selling.

CARMELITA

Ven Sophia, esto va a estar interesante.

SUBTITLE: Come Sophia, this is going to get interesting.

Carmelita clears a space for Sophia to come and join them. Sophia is not convinced. Carmelita changes her tactic. Sophia is seen unkempt, disheveled, with imprints of the jail bars on her suit.

CARMELITA (cont'd)

Wow. I've never seen you like this.

ORCHIDIA

Ni yo tampoco.

SUBTITLE: Me neither.

Carmelita takes a lipstick out of her breast.

CARMELITA

Hey, if you don't put some of this on they're never gonna let you out.

Sophia looks at herself, touching her hair, afraid that what Carmelita said might be true. She rushes to the cot to put lipstick on. All four are squeezed tight as they sit on the bench.

DEE

They called me hermana (sister). There was this gang—the Destroyers. They used to pick on this runt of a girl, Celia. They made her clean the floors and wash out their dirty underwear. She was a flunkie. Didn't talk much. Then they started beating up on her—I stuck up for her. She was Puerto Rican. So I got adopted by a Puerto Rican family. I belong to the Sandungueras. In prison, your family picks you. I was one of the six hermanas. María was mom. Josefa papá. She taught me salsa and merengue. Leticia was abuela, the peacemaker. You get adopted, you do better. It's good. When I first came in here, I was so drugged up I looked crazy. Nobody messed with me. Now things are real bad. Girls coming in are getting younger and they all got Uzis in the street. You can't act scared. You gotta act like you got a couple of bodies under your belt even if you don't, because some of them do. Prison's more violent now. Like the streets. But even in prison sometimes you get something. I'm a Sandunguera.

SOPHIA

Everywhere you go there's violence. Sometimes I just can't take it.

CARMELITA

I used to think that it was just us Latins who suffered from a more violent history—una vida ensangrentada (a life drenched in blood). It happened in our family to our Great-Aunt Cukita.

SOPHIA

Cukita?

14. EXTERIOR. PORCH. DAYTIME.

A short BLACK-AND-WHITE MOVIE in the style of a 1940s melodrama tells the story of Cukita. Cukita, the Long-Haired Woman, the Man in the White Suit, and the Ugly Man are played by the four principal actresses.

A woman is seen rocking in a rocking chair on a porch in a tropical country. She is Cukita. The film score is a tango in the style of Astor Piazzola.

Cukita bites her lips nervously. She is neurotic, anxious, hysterical, and rocks faster and faster in her chair.

SUPERIMPOSED TITLE: CUKITA.

The camera PANS from Cukita to a window next to her rocking chair. The window has bars.

14-A. INTERIOR. LIVING ROOM. DAYTIME.

LONG SHOT of the Long-Haired Woman playing the piano. She has very long hair and is not wearing any shoes. She plays the piano dramatically.

14-B. EXTERIOR. PORCH. DAYTIME.

The Man in the White Suit enters the porch. He is stout, dressed in a white linen suit and hat. He carries papers in his hand. He takes out his handkerchief and wipes his brow. Cukita sees him and smiles. The man is followed by the Ugly Man carrying a box of groceries. The man in the suit pats Cukita on the head, hands her an envelope, and walks into the house.

SUPERIMPOSED TITLE: CUKITA AN OLD MAID AT TWENTY-NINE.

The camera stays on Cukita as she opens the envelope and finds some dollar bills.

CLOSE-UP of money. Cukita clutches it and puts it into her bra.

The Ugly Man enters the porch where Cukita is rocking. He is wearing dark pants and shirt. He sweats heavily, especially under his arms, which show large stains. He is ugly and has greasy hair. He looks at Cukita.

Cukita, sensing his stare, is uncomfortable, and looks the other way.

He drops a ñame, a tuber common in the Caribbean. It lands close to Cukita's shoe.

They both stare at each other and the Ugly Man picks up the ñame.

CLOSE-UP of the ñame. The Ugly Man enters the house.

14-C. INTERIOR. LIVING ROOM. DAY.

The Long-Haired Woman is playing the piano. The Man in the White Suit sits watching, wiping the sweat from his brow.

14-D. INTERIOR. BATHROOM. DAY.

The Ugly Man is by the sink trying to clean his greasy hands, but they won't get clean. He looks at his face in the mirror and grimaces.

14-E. INTERIOR. LIVING ROOM. DAY.

The Man in the White Suit begins to have a heart attack. He is gagging and grasping at his shirt collar. The Long-Haired Woman at the piano stands up and screams.

14-F. EXTERIOR. PORCH. DAY.

Cukita stands up and runs inside the house.

14-G. INTERIOR. BATHROOM. DAY.

The Ugly Man looks in the direction of the screams and runs out of the bathroom.

14-H. INTERIOR. HALLWAY IN THE HOUSE. DAY.

The Ugly Man and Cukita run in slow motion toward the living room.

14-I. INTERIOR. ENTRANCE TO THE LIVING ROOM. DAY.

Cukita and the Ugly Man almost collide as they enter the living room. The Long-Haired Woman at the piano, Cukita, and the Ugly Man huddle around the Man in the White Suit who is having the heart attack.

POV OF THE STRICKEN MAN: the faces of Cukita, the Ugly Man and the Long-Haired Woman look distorted.

14-J. INTERIOR. HOSPITAL ROOM. NIGHT.

Cukita is crying as the Man in the White Suit lies in bed unconscious. The Ugly Man approaches her and suddenly drops to his knees. He grabs her legs and is trying to caress them but makes a run in her stockings with his greasy hands instead.

He puts his head on her lap and his greasy hair leaves a stain. Cukita is disgusted and tries to free herself from him. They struggle.

We can't tell anymore if they're struggling or in an amorous grip. The Ugly Man is about to kiss her. Her face shows horror. He takes out a gun and shoots her in the heart. Sound of gunshot. As she is falling he holds her gently and shoots himself in the heart. Another gunshot sound. Together they fall slowly to the ground.

14-K. NEWSPAPER HEADLINE.

We see a newspaper headline with blood dripping onto it. The headline reads: Unrequited Love: Woman Shot in Hospital. Killer then shoots himself. Cukita, an unmarried 29-year-old woman, was visiting her brother who had suffered a heart attack, when she was shot by Guillermo Pérez, 26 years old, who then shot himself. Mr. Pérez had been living with the family for six years. The victim, Cukita . . .

15. INTERIOR. PRISON.

Carmelita, Sophia, Dee, and Orchidia are all seen thinking. They look depressed. They are all sitting on the cot in a row. The camera PANS from one to the other as they talk.

SOPHIA

(shaking her head)

I never knew. All this time not knowing. Her pictures were all over the house, but if you mentioned her name, everyone just started crying.

ORCHIDIA

Always the same.

CARMELITA

Amor y violencia.

SUBTITLE: Love and violence.

DEE

Prisioneras del amor.

SUBTITLE: Women prisoners of love.

Dee utters the words as if it were the title of a popular song.

"Prisioneras del Amor," a song in the style of a heart-wrenching Mexican ranchera, comes on. What follows is an MTV-style production number in jail by Carmelita, Sophia, Dee, and Orchidia. Carmelita is dressed in a camouflage/Desert Storm flamenco costume, while the others are in camouflage pants and shirts that are opened, showing leopard-spotted bras underneath.

The dance includes them moving in a line, chain-gang-style, lunging at the bars as well as illustrating lyrics with gestures (e.g., when they sing "women prisoners of love," they clutch their hearts; "Love gives us warmth," they fan themselves; "Love gives us a great big pain," they caress their butts; "Making liberation our new religion," they make the sign of the cross and swig down shots of tequila.

ALL SING

Prisioneras del amor
Prisoneras de la vida
El amor nos da calor
Y también gran dolor

(Women prisoners of love
Women prisoners of life
Love gives us comfort and warmth
and also a great big pain)

Cambiaremos estas lágrimas y este llanto
Por fuerza, músculo, y sudor
Luchando siempre unidas
Abriéndonos las puertas
Para no ser más.

(We'll exchange our tears and sobs
for strength, muscle, and sweat
united in the struggle
opening doors for each other
so we'll never be again)

Prisioneras del amor
Prisioneras de la vida
Prisioneras de una historia
Una historia que nos borra
Y que nos quita el valor
de ser mujer.

(Women prisoners of love
women prisoners of life
prisoners of a history
that erases us
that takes away our worth as women)

Rompiéndonos los hábitos
De monjas enclaustradas
Haciendo que la liberación
Sea nuestra nueva religión.

(Tearing away at our habits
of cloistered nuns
making liberation
our new religion)

CLOSE-UP of all, holding onto the bars with TITLE SUPERIMPOSED: SING ALONG. This ranchera-style song is very soulful and they all end up saddened.

Prisioneras del amor
Prisioneras de la vida
El amor nos da calor
Y también un gran dolor.

CARMELITA

We need the spirit of Rosa.

SOPHIA

Rosa?

CARMELITA

Rosa Parks. She don't get up for a white man on the bus.

Their mood changes to one of excited optimism.

CARMELITA (cont'd)

She say:

Carmelita snaps her fingers and they begin to harmonize like a barbershop quartet that eventually turns into a fifties-style dance.

ORCHIDIA

Open that door wide.

SOPHIA

(belting out and cutting loose)

Baby come on out
Baby come on out
Drop that ball and chain
Drop that ball and chain
Drop that ball and chain

Sophia dances with Carmelita and Orchidia and with a limping Dee.

A Lawyer in a pants suit and short-cropped hair is seen standing near the door. They are dancing and don't see her until she whistles. They stop and rush to the door.

ORCHIDIA

Bonnie!

CARMELITA

(to Sophia)

I told you G.I.A. would come.

Bonnie's POV: All of the women except Dee are seen holding onto the bars.

Bonnie, a very butch lawyer, takes out papers from her briefcase. MEDIUM SHOT of Bonnie in front of the bars, holding papers.

BONNIE

What a day. You're the last of the 150 arrests. I can hardly see straight.

Sophia snickers and Carmelita elbows her.

BONNIE (cont'd)

I don't know what's going on here. Dictator gave me three names, but the cops are giving me four. Who is Cordelia Strong?

CARMELITA & ORCHIDIA

Cordelia?

BONNIE

Did she get arrested with you guys?

They turn and look at Dee. Dee shrugs.

CARMELITA

She did.

Orchidia goes to Dee on the cot and slaps a G.I.A. sticker on her.

ORCHIDIA

Qué hambre.

SUBTITLE: I'm starving.

CARMELITA

Empowerment makes you hungry.

ORCHIDIA

Does anyone have money?

SOPHIA

What a question. You fight and I pay.

Carmelita puts her arm around Sophia and takes out lipstick from her breast. She threatens Sophia with the lipstick. CLOSE-UP of the lipstick.

CARMELITA

Sophia, Invítala o te pinto.

SUBTITLE: Invite her or I'll smear you with my lipstick.

Sophia turns around.

CLOSE-UP of Cordelia.

SOPHIA

Cordelia . . . vente.

SUBTITLE: Cordelia, come with us.

CLOSE-UP of prison door opening as they are walking out. We see them from behind.

CARMELITA

Sophia, I forgot to tell you something. . . . Remember our father?

SOPHIA

The man who visits us every seven years?

CARMELITA

Well, he called to give us a surprise. We have a brother. Pepito. Eight years old.

16. EPILOGUE. INTERIOR. THEATER. NIGHT.

Thunderous applause is heard. Camera opens up on Pepito, a small Chinese boy with a quick smile on his face.

CLOSE-UP of front row of the theater: We see Pepito with his sister Sophia.

CLOSE-UP of Carmelita onstage.

CARMELITA

Damas y caballeros, ladies and gentlemen, I'd like to dedicate this song to an hermana Sandunguera who just passed away. She was H.I.V. and very positive. An inspiration to us all.

17. EXTERIOR. CASITA. DAY.

CLOSE-UP of Dee coming out of a house with ducks. She is dressed in flowery pants, a tight top, and big flashy earrings like Carmelita's. She carries fumigating equipment. The camera follows her as she gets on a truck with HERMANAS EXTERMINATING CO. emblazoned on its side. She smiles and gives a thumbs-up. FREEZE FRAME as the truck pulls away.

CARMELITA (voice-over)

From drugs to macrobiotic; from homelessness to a beautiful little house; from joblessness to executive businesswoman entrepreneur. This is for you, Dee.

18. INTERIOR. THEATER. NIGHT.

From a HIGH-ANGLE SHOT we see Carmelita's head bowing. She appears to be hit by roses thrown at her rather hard. Fade out as we hear thunderous applause and the beginning of "Prisioneras del Amor." End credits roll.

The End

Short Performance Scripts and Essays

The Conquest of Mexico as Seen through the Eyes of Hernán Cortés's Horse

by Carmelita Tropicana and Uzi Parnes (excerpt)

MY FIRST BATTLE

It was late afternoon and Thunder and I were having a hard time grazing. There was a cloud of mosquitoes hanging over us, buzzing, biting; it was unbearable. There were never this many killer mosquitoes in Spain. There were too many of them and we couldn't swat them fast enough with our tails. We shook as much as we could. We were so busy with the mosquitoes, we didn't listen to the meeting going on in my master's tent. My master and his captains came out of the tent in a hurry. Everybody got busy. They looked like busy ants. Soldiers were grabbing armor, muskets, shields. We were quickly saddled. My master mounted me. I could hear people moving behind us. I wanted to look behind but my master would have none of that. We took a few steps forward. Everybody got quiet. We circled and faced the crowd. Everyone was in line formations. Horsemen in front, foot soldiers behind. My master was not only my master; he was master of all these soldiers. I stood erect, tail high.

My master spoke: "Our scouts tell us warriors have been sighted beyond the hill. Though they are superior in numbers, we are superior in strength and power. Let us place our trust in Almighty God, who will protect us."

He called for a priest and when the priest stretched his arms everyone looked down. I looked down also and saw a chameleon scurrying past my hoofs. I was unfamiliar with some of the creatures in the New World. I had to learn which were good, which bad. Chameleons and cucarachas good, scorpions and mosquitoes bad.

The priest was handed a cross which he stuck in the ground. He gave a blessing: "Que Dios todopoderoso los guíe y dé protección en la lucha por la justicia en la conquista de América. Amen."

My master commanded: "Two shots will signal our attack. To the glory of God, to the glory of Spain."

Off we went, trotting towards the hill. I was excited but nervous.

I hate gunfire. It makes me jumpy. We broke into a gallop. When we reached the bottom of the hill Thunder and I heard something.

Beyond the hill. We pricked up our ears and snorted to each other. This was trouble. We looked at each other, slowing down to a trot. Our masters kicked us to pick up speed. When we got to the top of the hill, we couldn't believe our eyes. With our 340-degree peripheral vision all we could see were Indians. My master shot twice. I was startled, and reared up on my hind legs. Javelins, arrows whizzing by us. Guns firing. I was confused. We could get hurt. I'd never been in battle before. My master, upset, pulled the reins. He commanded. His tone angry: "Arriero. Arriero." My heart beat fast. I was sweating, my master knew. He knew where to go, what to do. He is my master. I listened, left, right, left again. I paid attention only to him, to his commands. Not to the javelins, swords, arrows, cannons blasting. It was all so loud. And fast. And everything got faster. My master got confident, he charged me through the crowds, groaning as he swiftly sliced heads, arms. The heads rolling down fields like melons, arms flying like birds. Alvarado yelled: "Die, you savages, rot in hell."

This went on for hours. My master's weight was beginning to weigh heavy on my back. I needed a back rub. This was my first battle and it was hard work. The fighting began to slow down. We were exhausted, but they were dead. So many dead Indians. The fight ended. The few Indians left alive gave up. My master spoke: "From this day forward you will be the subjects of His Majesty the King of Spain. In accepting him as your lord, you will obtain many favors from His Majesty, who will help defend you from your enemies. So be it."

As I looked at the bodies in the field, the last stars were disappearing. I thought of my mother's farewell words the day I left Spain: "Arriero, from now on you will be counting stars in the New World." No mother, not stars.

THE NIGHTMARE

My master and I were inseparable. I stayed a few feet from the tent where he slept. Often I saw the candle in his tent burning late into the night. I remembered how he had gotten very serious one day as he was coming out of the tent and had told Alvarado: "Our salvation lies in God and our horses." "God and our horses" echoed in my head as I closed my eyes at night.

One day messengers came and went. A horse senses when things are not right. Just as horses can find water in the desert, a horse knows when danger approaches.

I rotated my left ear and heard one of his captains say he had seen rocks stored on rooftops in the town of Cholula, and the roads were blocked. My master said, "We must surprise them. And teach them a lesson. I want you to ask fifty of the highest ranking chiefs to come to our camp for a summit."

When the chiefs came, my master ordered his men to arrest them. A few minutes later I was saddled. I heard him tell Alvarado we were going to Cholula. I would rather have stayed grazing a couple of more hours than go to battle. I looked around. We weren't taking any cannons or foot soldiers, and the priest didn't come to give us a blessing. No, it wasn't a battle. I was relieved. I nickered a greeting to my master as he mounted me.

The race to Cholula was exhilirating. The night had a gentle breeze. It was about two in the morning. I soon passed Thunder and Volador, two of the fastest horses. I didn't think I could, but then when you have a master like Hernán Cortés, you do things you don't think possible. I remember the day he chose me. He looked me in the eyes, he smelled of beef stew, which I hate; I'm a vegetarian. But quickly he said: "Are you the best? You have to be the best if you are to be the horse of Hernán Cortés." And he smacked me on the rump. The way he said it, I wanted to be the best. He had a way of making everyone do the impossible. When we were crossing the desert and we were all exhausted, hungry, thirsty, we'd hear him say: "Adelante cristianos, a la gloria de Dios." And that kept us going. Men and horses.

He rode me so well, the Cempoal Indians said we looked like one. He knew just how to give commands with a simple tug at the reins; his heels would dig into me just right. I listened to his voice, deep and forceful. I was proud to be the horse of Hernán Cortés, the conquistador.

As we approached Cholula, I thought we should slow down, but no, our speed continued. One Indian was near the entrance carrying a bundle on his head. Two shots were fired and he fell. There was a loud sound coming from a tower. We entered the town at full speed. People came out onto the streets. They looked confused. We shot at them. We took a turn through a narrow street. Children and women came running out naked. It was so narrow and we were going so fast I couldn't stop. I trampled on them with my hoofs. I didn't want to, but it was so fast. After that street my master whipped me like he had never whipped me before. I heard screams and the sound of my hoofs on the ground. My master set torches on fire and threw them on roofs, inside houses. I hate fire as much as as gunfire. We kept going, torching. I couldn't understand this battle; there were hardly any arrows thrown at us, no warriors. We didn't seem to be in danger. When we got back to the camp there was a wounded horse and his master lying side-by-side. They were pouring hot oil on their wounds. Would I one day be lying side-by-side with my master? I was parched with thirst. I was drinking from a large bucket of water, when I heard bloodcurdling screams. All fifty chiefs came out of a tent bleeding. Their hands had been cut off. All fifty chiefs had no hands.

Two days later I fell sick with influenza. I was very sick. Some liquid was poured on my tongue. I broke out in a sweat, a fever raged. What visions I had that night. Over and over I kept trampling on children and then when I looked at my hoofs, my hoofs were cut off, I could no longer gallop.

When I got well again I thought I had only dreamt about what happened in Cholula and about the chiefs with their hands cut off, that it was all a nightmare. Or was it? Maybe things would change, maybe that would be the end of our fury.

Two weeks later we set off to the city called Tenochtitlán.

Performance Art Manifesto

Carmelita Tropicana

I know you will not sleep tonight, tossing and turning, tossing and turning, thinking, How did she become a performance artist? So I tell you.

I became a performance artist in 1987 when a filmmaker by the name of Ela Troyano called me up and said there was a grant given by the New York Foundation for the Arts for performance art. I said, "Ela, performance art?" She said, "Five thousand dollars." I said, "Performance art, of course." So I rushed right over and write in the application "deconstruction, deconstruction, deconstruction." I know they like that word. So what do you know, I got the grant. So I have a piece of advice for all you girls out there: Do it, do it, and then you find out what the heck it is. A posteriori, a priori, whatever.

So now that I was a performance artist, I had to put together my own *Performance Art Manifesto,* which I would like to share with you. I will begin with definitions.

The first definition is by a famous performance artist, she is short, with short hair, a musician that goes "Ooh, ooh, ooh." That's right: Laurie Anderson. Laurie Anderson says, and I quote: "Performance art is performance by a live artist." This is true. If the artist is dead it is not performance art.

The second definition is by another performance artist who is short, with short hair, who was defunded by the National Endowment for the Arts for the homoerotic content in her work, the infamous Holly Hughes. And Holly says, and I quote: "Ninety percent of performance art is in the costumes." Voilà, check out my camouflage, Desert Storm, rumba, and flamenco dancer costume.

The third definition is by another performance artist who is short, with short hair, and who wears camouflage outfits. Yes, it is me, and I quote myself. Performance art changes the way you look at the world. Your perceptions are changed; an object is no longer what it seems.

Exhibit number one. (Showing a toilet plunger to audience) What is this, people? I ask you, eh? What did you say? A plunger? Hah. I laugh at you wildly. This is what I also thought this was, a plunger, until I saw a performance artist by the name of Jack Smith. The performance was in the Greenwich Village in a concrete basement. It was packed, there were eight of us. There was a breeze created by fans on the floor and beautiful Scheherazade music playing, when out came the exotic Jack Smith, dancing like an Arabian prince/princess in diaphanous material. In the middle of the concrete floor he poured gasoline to form a black lagoon. Then he took a match and set fire to the lagoon. The flames got bigger and bigger; we thought we were going to die in the conflagration. Jack relevéd, pliéd, and chasséd to the corner and took out this plunger and, never missing a beat in his dance, put out the flames. Ladies and gentlemen, I am a superintendent of a building and when a tenant calls me to tell me something is stuck in the toilet, I cannot hold this in my hands without thinking of Jack and his dance. And this plunger is no longer a plunger. It has been transformed. It is a "plunger" (pronouncing it with French accent). It is an objet d'art. An objet d'art.

I remember Jack Smith, who died of AIDS in 1989.

Radio Spot for WNYC

Carmelita Tropicana

The following spot was played between classical music selections.

Hello people, you know me, I know you. I don't need no American Express card, I am Carmelita Tropicana, superintendent, performance artist.

I love New York. It's always a thrill a minute. Just the other day I was walking home after a show and a tall stranger in the night got very close to me and pulled out a big magnum revolver and asked me for my purse. I am very nice, I don't tell him my gold lamé purse doesn't match his brown shoes, and I don't do this because I know people on crack are not polite like people on heroin. People on heroin are always nodding and bowing to you, very polite.

Well after my night of adventure I was ready for a day of quiet commune with nature, so off I went to the Brooklyn Botanical Gardens for a little aromatherapy. The roses were in bloom, the Tropicana rose next to the Audrey Hepburn. As I inhaled, a bird, a cardinal flew over my head, singing: (whistle) gun control, (whistle) gun control. What a sweet song.

This is Carmelita Tropicana, your cultural attaché.

El Recibo Social / The Social Visit

Carmelita Tropicana

One of the most entertaining times I ever had was visiting my great aunt María Angelina who was in the hospital dying. She was ninety-six.

Two days before the visit my mother had called to tell me María Angelina, whom we call Nina, had been rushed to the hospital. "This is it," she said. I thought of the many times we thought, "This is it," for Nina, and her two sisters, Pradina, who was my grandmother, and her sister Ludesvinda.

Twenty years ago, when Nina was leaving Cuba, the Cuban officials had also thought "this was it" for Nina as they drove her to the airport in an ambulance. Nina's two main ailments were a heart condition and a disease that had left her legs swollen like thick stumps. She came to the United States and settled with her sister Ludesvinda in Rhode Island, where she taught piano.

The family had always known that if "this is it" for one, the other two would closely follow. So tight was this triumvirate we referred to it as Las Tres Marías—for the three Marys present at Jesus Christ's crucifixion. They were born in Spain and never let you forget it. There were sixteen siblings but only nine made it to adulthood. Nina was the oldest of the girls, the caretaker, the one with the spirit. "Qué espíritu tiene!" everyone would say. With those legs of hers she can barely walk, but she's still cooking gourmet and teaching piano, and she bought a new VCR.

Las tres Marías were tight but critical. With three, power plays occurred and two would unite against one. My grandmother and Vinda would begin their session with: "Tú sabes como es Angelina—You know how Angelina is. Always with those aristocratic airs. Remember el recibo social, those Wednesday afternoon visits. Angelina didn't have a penny to her name but she insisted on these visits. Cuka Campa would come, driven by her chauffeur, along with other socialites. If Cuka Campa had come two hours earlier she would have seen Angelina on all fours scrubbing the marble floor for the visit. She's extreme with everything. She thinks it's gourmet, but she overspices and oversalts everything. And her insistence on food decoration, the lace, the embroidery. You'd think her turkey would get up and dance the minuette. Vinda, you're a better cook. And you, Pradina, are a better seamstress."

And then it would be Angelina and my grandmother's turn: "Tú sabes como es Vinda. You know how she is with her nerves. Who can forget those postpartum depressions, playing piano barefoot and wailing like Medea. And that long hair she has. I told her to cut it off; how can a woman her age be wearing a braid?"

And then Angelina and Vinda on my grandmother: "You know how Pradina is and will always be—domineering. Everyone has to do what she wants. Her husband and children have always been under her thumb. She had her husband well trained. He had to call her on the phone every five minutes to report where he was and what he was doing. No wonder they nicknamed him Ring-ring."

Nina, as the eldest, married first. She married Bernardo, a partner in a lucrative hardware store. In the early years of marriage, they took a whole year off to travel throughout Spain, landing in Puerto Pajares and going to the beaches of San Sebastián in the north of Spain. The couple journeyed inland by train to Madrid, Toledo, Sevilla. The trip was memorable in more ways than one. When they returned to Cuba her husband's partner in the hardware store had died, and his widow was suing Nina's husband for the business. The lawsuit with the evil widow dragged on for years. They never really recovered financially. The widow took most of it and Nina's husband Bernardo settled for a warehouse with some equipment.

That left Nina to fend for work, which she did very resourcefully, a government post here, a piano lesson there. Nina and Bernardo were childless, and Nina seemed content with nieces and a nephew. My mother's fondest childhood memories are of Sunday picnics with Nina at the cemetery. It'd be sunny, there were lots of trees. They'd buy flowers, scrub the family's mausoleum, make flower arrangements, and picnic. She recalls the time Nina and her husband had to give up everything, including their chauffeured car and driver Benjamin, and go live with them. Nina and Bernardo slept in cots in the living room for almost two years. It was crowded in the house. There was only one bathroom which my mother's brother, then thirteen, occupied all the time. He would sit with a rifle for hours, a BB gun aimed at a rat he had seen in the courtyard entering the maid's room. Hunting the rat consumed him. My grandfather was consumed with running his restaurant. The restaurant was on the corner and next to it was an empty house with a lot. Every night after nine P.M. a procession of waiters would cross the abandoned lot with dinner trays. By that time my mother said she was too hungry and tired to enjoy the meal. And then there were the fights between my grandfather and Bernardo. They'd yell across the dinner table "Franco is an SOB." "The republicans are the SOBs. They should all be hung." The wives would calm them down with "Politics is not good for the digestion."

It was at this time that my mother saw Nina get hysterical for the first time. Hysterics were usual occurrences for her sisters, but rare with Nina. It happened when Nina was cleaning a vase in the living room. The vase was a four-foot Chinese cloisonné vase brought over from Spain for my grandmother as a wedding gift from a high dignitary. When Nina accidentally knocked the vase over, the crash sent my grandmother rushing in screaming "El jarrón, el jarrón." Angelina, a lover of fine things, looked at the shards, sobbed uncontrollably and plummetted to the ground. My grandmother kept mentioning that jarrón for years.

On the phone I could sense my mother's discomfort with impending doom. She always says she felt closer to Nina than to her own mother. I felt decisive. "You should take off work," I said, "and we can go visit." I called my cousin to give her the news and she also said she'd take off work and visit. I called my sister who also said the same thing. So there we were taking a Greyhound bus to Rhode Island, going to the hospital for the day, chomping on Oreo cookies and ham-and-cheese sandwiches and gossiping enough for the three Marías to be proud.

Near the hospital we spotted a Latin luncheonette and stopped for steak and fried bananas. Food that's familiar is very comforting when this is it. We topped off the meal with the preferred beverage of the three sisters, café con leche.

As we entered the hospital, our aunt and uncle were exiting and they looked down and mumbled, "This is it." When I saw her lying in bed from the doorway I was a little shocked. She had lost weight. Her hair was uncoiffed; no rouge, powder, or lipstick. Not that she wore that much, but she always had a hint of color. We slowly entered and she opened her eyes. "There you are. I feel terrible. Look at all these tubes. In the middle of the night these men, these brutes, yanked me out of bed. What force they used on me. They handled me like an animal, like a bull being rent in two, I heard my bones crack. What excruciating pain. I screamed. I must have woken everybody up. All so they could put a tube in my heart. They were so brutal. I don't think I can take that pain again. I've made my peace. I have. Look at me, I got tubes everywhere, a tube in my nose, a tube in my throat, a tube in my heart, and a tube in my crotch." "I guess we'll call you tuberías," said my mother. "Don't make me laugh, Nenita. Come sit down. You look as young as ever, but your mother. What is the matter with her? She talks such nonsense. I called her three weeks ago, she didn't know who I was. The stupid things she said. I can't believe it. But how are you?"

One by one we give Nina a condensed version of our lives. My mother goes first. She is still working at the Spanish TV station on 55th Street, which is convenient when she gets a call from my grandmother's home attendant with a medical emergency: asthma attack, a fall, a stroke. She can always run to my grandmother's on 59th Street. Between medicines and Pampers, from 55th to 59th Street. My sister goes next. She talks about her independent filmmaking, a lot of control, little money. She has a project with a rap group and did break up with her boyfriend, but doesn't mention the new one. Then it's my turn. I re-enact a commercial I did and sing a couple of bars from a song I have in a musical. Nina asks: "Whatever happened to that boyfriend you had?" I go into a reverie of the tall blond woman I'm seeing. My sister rearranges Nina's pillow and says, "She's too busy with her career." Then goes my cousin. She still works at the coffee export place, finally broke up with her boyfriend everyone hated, but she's got a new one everyone likes. Nina asks about the possibility of a wedding. My cousin says it'll be some time in the summer. Nina has to come. So we all fantasize about what she will wear. Nina starts to describe ensembles she wore to previous weddings, a wedding in 1928, one in '35, another in '48. She describes an ostrich-feather hat she wore to one wedding. My mother recalls the wedding. She was six years old and she and her brother, left unsupervised, dipped into the punch-bowl too many times. In the middle of the night they both vomited on themselves. Nina said: "You couldn't hold your liquor, but you were my favorite."

"La Chata, the pimples you used to get and mange from sleeping with those alley cats. You were so skinny." "That's why guys used to yell at you: 'Toma Kresto. Drink chocolate milk.' They never would have yelled that if they'd seen you in the gown I made for your fifteenth birthday. You looked ravishing." The dress was a salmon taffeta and the full long skirt was made of multilayered leaves, each one individually cut and sewn and painted sparingly with gold paint to simulate veins. The sleeves were full and fluffy. To Nina my mother must have been a young bud rising from all this foliage, but a bud that had been stuffed on top with a lot of Kleenex. The dress had passed down to posterity courtesy of photographs taken at the exclusive Alembert studios. One pose has my mother leaning against Doric columns. Like a young starlet, she casually holds a feathered cape that trails on the ground. In another pose my mother sits on wide steps, the skirt cascading down. The dress vied with the cake for pièce de résistance and was another Nina fantasy design. It was shaped into a rectangle and there was a square left in the middle where there was a mirror simulating a lake. On top of the mirror sat a basket adorned with sweetheart roses. There were pink ribbons attached to the center of the basket. At the stroke of midnight, the guests, all teenagers in evening wear, gathered around the cake. My mother blew out the candles and the guests pulled on the ribbons. The basket opened and two turtledoves flew out. Actually, Nina remembers one had to be pushed out. They circled the room, the sound of their wings flapping mixed with the sighs the oohs and aahs of the guests until finally they found the window and the doves disappeared into Havana's midnight sky. The fifteenth birthday or, as they were called, los quince were fiercely competitive, and families battled one another for who could put on the best show.

My mother still bears a grudge. "If it hadn't been for Nina, I wouldn't have had a party. My own mother wouldn't celebrate it." Nina explains that my grandmother was too upset; her husband had left for Venezuela to set up a business, and times were hard.

Hard times reminds my mother of the monthly calls by the bill collector from Fin de Siglo, Havana's Bloomingdale. "What was his name?" Nina answers: "Yglesias. He looked like César Romero with dark curly hair and mustache. He was so neat. He'd open his briefcase and take out folders for the three of us." My mother says whenever he came they'd act as if it were a surprise. "Señor Yglesias, you didn't tell us you were coming today. If you had I would have made your favorite dessert, las tres leches. I'm afraid I only have arroz con leche. Ludesvinda, make a fresh pot of coffee while I entertain Mr. Yglesias. He takes it light and sweet. What an elegant tie you have." My mother says he'd have coffee and dessert, and often not get paid.

I realize how Nina has changed from the moment we come into the room. With all her tubes she's the one doing most of the talking. She puts us up-to-date on family matters—who's getting married, divorced, who's still drinking, and she covers all the relatives in the northeastern corridor from Massachusetts to Florida. She then switches to opera and starts to describe the plot of *Aida*. In the middle, a woman and a boy who's about twelve come in. Nina introduces us and the woman is happy: we are the relatives from New York, the ones she's always hearing about. To prove it she tells my mother she lives on 59th Street, and we are artists. Nina calls the boy who tentatively takes a step forward. "This is Luis, my best student ever." Luis's ears get red. "Have you been practicing *Los Estudios* de Chopin and Liszt's *Hungarian Rhapsody* like I told you and not that rock? You know what you have to do if you want to get my piano." The mother tells Nina a mass was offered in her name and asks if we mind if she prayed now. She takes Nina's hand and the boy echoes the prayers. We watch. It feels like we are voyeurs. New York heathens. Watching people pray devoutly is a rare sight. I watch Luis whose behavior is so respectful and formal he seems to have entered Nina's time. I realize as I say good-bye to Nina that I am saying good-bye to her time. I hear the *Comparsa* de Lecuona, *Les Études* of Chopin, *Sevilla* of Albéniz playing on a cream-colored baby grand piano. Good-bye to the matriarchy that ushered in the twentieth century, Nina born in 1896.

Good-bye to Las Tres Marías and a dessert called las tres leches.

Good-bye to women who sew their own clothes and value beautiful penmanship;

Good-bye to women who wear nylon hose and hair nets and would never dream of going out without lipstick, powder, and a bit of rouge;

Good-bye to women drinking café para quitarse la debilidad y entonarse el estomago;

Good-bye to women who upheld the sanctity of marriage and stuck with their husbands through economic depressions, extramarital affairs, alcoholism, prison;

Good-bye to women, those coquettes with salacious double entendres sitting in rocking chairs in late afternoons fanning themselves and checking in on their neighbors' affairs;

Good-bye to women born in Spain living in Cuba who never traded the Spanish *z* for the Cuban *s*;

Good-bye to women who know how to celebrate special occasions with recitations of poems from the classical Sor Juana "la que peca por la paga" o "el que paga por pecar" as well as their own composition, María Angelina's own Ode to herself on the eve of her ninetieth birthday;

Good-bye to fanciful cakes with turtledoves flying into the twinkling Havana sky.

Nina was so much of her time, but kept up with ours by buying a VCR.

Luis and his mother leave. We are left to say good-bye to Nina. It's been three hours. With her gravelly voice she says adiós. We kiss her. The visit feels complete. Like watching an artist who's finished her canvas and is signing her name with bold and flowery letters, María Angelina Canales Viuda de Blanco.

After Nina died her sisters closely followed. I inherited Nina's dessert plate, the one she used for las tres leches.

Food for Thought

Carmelita Tropicana

I am an artist, a very, very sensitive person. I suffer a lot from angst. But when I get this angst attack, I turn to the three arts: poetry, macramé, and cooking. Food can elevate, inspire, ennoble. The noble Nobel laureate Pablo Neruda wrote "Ode to the Lemon," "Ode to the Artichoke," "Ode to Olive Oil." A man with a good appetite, rotund, chunky, not an anorexic poet. He used food to feed his poetry for the lofty purpose of Art. Oh Pablito! Others, however, have done the opposite. Food has dragged them down to the muck and mire, unleashed the beast in their belly. Take Dr. Tarnower and Jean. Everyone who has been on the Scarsdale diet knows that the good doctor was not murdered because of unrequited love. It was all those carrots, celery, and lettuce he made Jean eat. It was too much roughage for her. And Harvey Milk was another example of where food has played a meaty role. He was murdered by a man who said he ate too many Twinkies. Since then I have stopped eating them lest I turn on my brothers and sisters and also kill the current mayor of the city of New York.

Two months ago my girlfriend insulted me. She called me a food slut. A food slut! I had to think. I was thinking and thinking so much I became an intellectual. Was it true? Was it caused by my genes or by my culture? My grandfather had had many restaurants. My grandmother was a great cook. And it is true I came from a strong food culture. I was born in Cuba. In Cuba when you do something good you say: te la comiste. You ate it. If you are despicable you are mala leche—bad milk. When a musician plays real good we yell azúcar, azúcar—sugar. Genitals are referred to as fruit, papaya, or as bread, bollo. A lesbian is a tortillera, a lover of tortillas. A man with a big chorizo, sausage, is held in high esteem.

The insult led me to examine my relationship to food. I underwent therapy, hypnosis, started memory recall. There was that incident in 1984 when I took cooking lessons from the Honorable Benihana San. I combined the mystery of the Orient with the flavor of the Spanish and created my masterpiece, the chicken sushi. Why had I combined these two cuisines? Was this a precursor to the multiculti revolution? What has food meant to me, to us, throughout the ages? I had to know. I was a mad scientist, insatiable in my food quest.

The proof was in the pudding. Spain has great bread pudding. England has Yorkshire pudding. I began with the colonizers and explorers. Columbus came from strong food cultures, Italy and Spain. He had good food. Why, then, did he come to America? Was he looking for gold? Was he looking for converts to Christianity? No. He was looking for spices. A little pepper and hot sauce to make his Spanish omelet zing with pizzazz. He was looking for new and improved taste. The British colonizers were different. They did not have a strong food culture. They were desperate. They left England to escape overcooked veggies and Marmite. Eureka! I was on to something.

To my historical thinking I added a dollop of geography. I discovered that sometimes people we associate with a particular food are not the originators of that food. You say potato, I say the Irish, until I stepped into the civilization of the Incas, master builders of Machu Picchu, and found a people who cultivated many, many different kinds of potatoes. How exciting to learn that they had dehydrated potatoes millennia before NASA did. I couldn't contain my thrill when I found out they had a museum in Peru devoted only to the potato. And if you said potato and I said potato what about the tomato? Italians can pay homage to the indigenous people of the Americas who presented them with their natural treasure, the golden apple they call pomodoro, which they have raised to celestial Bolognese glory. And I cannot leave out the Yankee doodle dandies on the 4th of July grilling their hamburgers, hot dogs, and portobello mushrooms. They gotta thank the Arawaks of the Caribbean who invented the barbacoa they call BBQ.

This was a lot of thinking. I was ready for action. I had to experiment. Open sesame. I took a bagel, schmeared it with cream cheese, laced it with lox and slivers of red onion, added a bit of lemon juice, and powdered it with fresh ground pepper. I bit it. Clearly from that first bite I could say I had the utmost admiration for the Jewish people. But it didn't stop there. I did a trinity dip with hot puffy poori, from dahl to nuanced chicken curry sauce to sweet mango chutney. Indian food rules! But what about food presentation? After all, I am an artist. It was time to ingest an artfully wrapped morsel. Seaweed hugging a pillow of rice with a surprising mackerel in the middle, which I anointed with sinus-clearing mustard and to which I added pink ginger. Arigato. I bow to the Japanese. My thoughts were popping like kernels of corn from these experiments. If eyes are the windows of the soul, then the mouth is the door, the entrée to love and understanding of a people. Surely we can begin to know a people through their food. Food can bind and bond us globally like Chinese rice. The individual glutinous grains sticking to one another until a bed is created, a bed we can all lie in peacefully, the lion with the lamb, the chicken with the shrimp.

What I was missing was the psychological angle to food. Throughout history there has been fear of foreign food. There's the fear of the white fish chub in the deli. How would you eat it? It doesn't look so good. Where's the meat? Then there is the fear of mole sauce. Chocolate and chicken? That sounds very strange. And cashew juice. How can you squeeze a nut? How do Brazilians do it? I confess to having had all the above fears. But I overcame them. I opened wide. You have to be open. If you close yourself you will succumb to your fears. You may even be dragged down collectively into the muck and mire like the people in California who voted for the anti-immigration legislation, Proposition 187. They had a big fear. Fear of the tortillas. In voting for it they have denied the enrichment that an immigrant group can have on a culture. There is a Yoruba saying for people with food phobias, you are like fried fish. You have one eye open but you cannot see.

From the political I have come back to the personal. I know the way to a girl's heart is through the stomach and so did my girlfriend. So I invited her over and in the spirit of love and understanding made her an arroz con pollo, a chicken with rice to die for. One taste and she swooned in ecstasy like Saint Teresa in the statue by Bernini. And I was her little Cupid who pierced her with my arrow, an arrow of arroz con pollo, and she fell into la petite morte. Who was the food slut now?

Arroz con Pollo (Chicken with Rice)

1 breast of chicken, split, and 2 thighs (skinless)
1 large onion
3–4 garlic cloves
1 green pepper
1 cup crushed tomatoes or 8-ounce can
¼ teaspoon oregano
1 teaspoon basil

pepper to taste
Sazón Goya
1 cube beef bouillon
1 cup red wine
1 cup rice and 1½ cups of water
1 small can pimentos
1 small can petit pois
a small piece of sausage (Spanish-style cantinpalo, but any sausage will do in a pinch)

Acknowledgments

I am very grateful to my collaborators Ela Troyano and Uzi Parnes, who generously agreed to include the various fruits of our labor in this tome. I share this book with them.

I would also like to express my gratitude to my editor Chon Noriega and to Micah Kleit of Beacon Press.

A number of academics have provided invaluable criticism: José Esteban Muñoz, David Roman, Alicia Arrizón, Lillian Manzor, Yvonne Yarbro Bejerano, Jill Dolan, Diana Taylor, Alberto Sandoval and Larry La Fountain.

The following theatres and presenting arts organizations have been instrumental in the development of my work: Ellie Covan of Dixon Place, Mark Russell, Luxy Sexton and Lynn Moffatt as well as the board and staff of Performance Space 122, David White of Dance Theatre Workshop, Abe Rybeck of The Theatre Offensive, Max Ferra, Maria Irene Fornes, Jim Lewis, Graciela Daniele, Luis Santeiro whom I met at Intar, and all the women of WOW.

I thank my family, friends and colleagues for their support: Ela Dopazo, Patricia Dopazo, Gerry Gomez Pearlberg, Nely Galan, Holly Hughes, Peggy Shaw, Lois Weaver, Maureen Angelos, Madeleine Olnek, Kate Stafford, Sharon Jane Smith, Eileen Myles, Lisa Kron, Dona Ann McAdams, Peggy Healey, Babs Davy, Diane Jeep Ries, Helen Frankenthal, Ana María Simo, Kelly Cogswell, Mary Patierno, Cathy Quinlan, Diane Rodríguez, Luis Alfaro, Fernando Rivas, Jurgen Brunning, Suzanne Pillsbury, Dolores Prida, Lorraine Llamas, Alfredo Bejar, Jennifer Monson, Lawrenzo Heit, Burt Harris, Nicole Mitchell, Sandra Meyers, Guinevere Turner, Rebecca Sumner Burgos, Ana Margaret Sánchez, Annie Iobst, Ari Gold, Henry Gifford, Susan Muska, Greta Olafsdottir, Charles Scott Richard, Jane Di Kron, Lori E. Seid, Susan Cahan, Kathleen McHugh, Thelma Price, Raul Lanio, Jack Smith and Rafik.

CARMELITA TROPICANA: Your Kunst Is Your Waffen
A film by Ela Troyano
1994, 28:00, 16mm, color
Produced in association with THE INDEPENDENT TELEVISION SERVICE (ITVS) Executive Producer and Director: Ela Troyano, Line Producer: Alfredo Bejar. Screenplay: Carmelita Tropicana and Ela Troyano. Production Design: Uzi Parnes. Cinematographer: Sarah Cawley. Music: Fernando Rivas. Editor: Freddie Rodriguez. Featuring: Carmelita Tropicana, Sophia Ramos, Anne Iobst, and Livia Daza Paris. Additional funding: New York State Council on the Arts.

1994 selected festivals with filmmaker in attendance
Rimini International Film Festival; Toronto International Film Festival; San Francisco International Lesbian and Gay Film Festival; Set In Motion, NYSCA's Retrospective, Lincoln Center; New Festival, New York Lesbian and Gay Film Festival; Chicago Latino Cine Festival; Torino, Festival Internazionale di Film; Berlin International Film Festival.

Awards
1994 Berlin International Film Festival
Teddy Bear for Best Short Film
1994 San Francisco International Lesbian & Gay Film Festival
Stolichnaya Rising Star Award; Audience Award for Best Short

Distribution
Public television premiere June 1995; PBS release with ITVS's "American Independents" series in 1996.

Theatrical release with Tomás Gutierréz Alea's *Strawberry and Chocolate* throughout Germany, September 1995, with its star, Carmelita Tropicana, introducing the film.

Theatrical and video release in a program of Lesbian Shorts, "Girlfriends," July 1996, by First Run Features.